THE MARTYR'S CONVICTION
A Sociological Analysis

Program in Judaic Studies
Brown University
BROWN JUDAIC STUDIES
Edited by
Jacob Neusner, Ernest S. Frerichs, William Scott Green,
Wendell S. Dietrich, Calvin Goldscheider, David Hirsch, Alan Zuckerman

Project Editors (Projects)

David Blumenthal, Emory University (Approaches to Medieval Judaism)
William Brinner (Studies in Judaism and Islam)
Ernest S. Frerichs, Brown University (Dissertations and Monographs)
Lenn Evan Goodman, University of Hawaii (Studies in Medieval Judaism)
William Scott Green, University of Rochester (Approaches to Ancient Judaism)
Norbert Samuelson, Temple University (Jewish Philosophy)
Jonathan Z. Smith, University of Chicago (Studia Philonica)

Number 203
THE MARTYR'S CONVICTION

by
Eugene Weiner
and
Anita Weiner

THE MARTYR'S CONVICTION
A Sociological Analysis

by

Eugene Weiner
and
Anita Weiner

Scholars Press
Atlanta, Georgia

THE MARTYR'S CONVICTION

© 1990
Brown University

Library of Congress Cataloging-in-Publication Data

Weiner, Eugene.
    The martyr's conviction : a sociological analysis / by Eugene
Weiner and Anita Weiner.
    p. cm. -- (Brown Judaic studies ; no. 203)
    Includes bibliographical references.
    ISBN 1-55540-435-9 (alk. paper)
    1. Martyrdom. 2. Martyrs--Psychology. 3. Belief and doubt.
4. Religion and sociology. I. Weiner, Anita. II. Title.
III. Series.
BL626.5.W45 1989
302.5'4--dc20   89-48209
                                        CIP

Printed in the United States of America
on acid-free paper

Dedication

To Hanna: To what could have been but wasn't.

The Martyr's Conviction: A Sociological Analysis

TABLE OF CONTENTS

Acknowledgments

We are particularly indebted to our son, Dr. David Weiner, who read the manuscript and has given us useful advice throughout the various stages of research and writing. He contributed significantly to the formulation of Chapter Two, "Conviction and Social Types; The Origins of Classical Martyrdom." At the Psycho-History Association in Wellfleet, Massachusetts we had the pleasure of presenting our work with David, and we benefited there from the helpful comments of Robert J. Lifton, Erik H. Erikson, Norman Birnbaum, Kai Erikson and Harvey Cox. B.J. Lifton's work on the martyrdom of Janusz Korczak was also helpful in focusing our conceptual framework on a concrete historical instance.

There were many Institutes and Libraries which were important and helpful during the years of gathering information. In London, the staff of the Courtland Institute Galleries was gracious as we made our way through their paintings of martyrs. The Warburg Institute concretized for us the vastness of martyrologies, and the staff of the Wiener Library was helpful in locating and making available the martyrological Nazi propaganda. We used the facilities of the British Museum Library searching for martyrs, and our time spent there was particularly useful. In New York, we profited from the days spent in the Jung Institute searching for symbolic meanings, and are grateful to the staff at the Union Theological Seminary Library for their helpfulness. Bibliographic searches were done at the University of Toronto Library with efficiency and consideration.

We are grateful to Gerson Cohen of the Jewish Theological Seminary of America who encouraged us to search for conviction in the Acts of martyrological self-sacrifice. His conversation with us, years back, set us on our way.

And finally, we are indeed grateful to our academic home, Haifa University, which has provided us with the privileged security within which we can follow our interests.

Eugene Weiner
Anita Weiner

Mt. Carmel, Haifa, Israel, 1989

Introduction

Martyrdom: The Social Construction of Conviction

This is a book about the linkage between convictions and the willingness to die for them, between the belief in a cause and the willingness to commit oneself totally to it. Conviction[1] is necessary in human life. It gives meaning to the course of human existence, and provides answers to the central questions of life.

In the modern western world, the psychological climate discourages total commitment and martyrdom. Individuals willing to martyr themselves for a cause strike us as irrational and motivated by psychological problems. Their convictions do not appear to be the expressions of free will and considered judgement. In an age of loosening communal and family ties, the individual who is irrevocably committed to particular convictions seems needlessly inflexible.

In addition, so many people have been sacrificed for what appear to be stupidities, that there is considerable suspicion about the sacrifice of life for any cause. This is the age of the "martyrs of Jonestown," and the bloody martyrs of Khomeini. Consequently the act of sacrifice often generates in us a feeling of despair at the waste of precious life. This is particularly true in an age when "conviction contests" have become too dangerous. The stakes are too high. Viewing adversaries as

---

[1]We have found the definition of conviction by James Wm. McClendon Jr. and James M. Smith, *Understanding Religious Convictions* (1975) most helpful. "Convictions are persistent beliefs, such that if X (a person or a community) has a conviction, it will not be easily relinquished without making X a significantly different person or community than before." p. 7. Convictions differ from attitudes and beliefs in their persistence over time; the degree to which they influence other beliefs; and the way they are integrative in and constitutive of personhood and community. These are the characteristics that make convictions so difficult to adjudicate.

representatives of Evil Empires may bolster our morale, but they create the conditions for a showdown which could destroy the world.

How can anyone still believe in causes when the twentieth century has been witness to a series of the most horrendous mass murders in the name of worthy principles? People are rightfully suspicious of the moral demands of causes. For modern sensibilities, the martyr's dramatic struggle between good and evil, between victory and defeat appear to be the conflicts of the stage, not the stuff of everyday life.

If convictions are too dangerous, perhaps we should learn to live with our less binding and improvised attitudes and beliefs instead. The social sciences are constantly collecting and analyzing information collected from attitude surveys, and we know a good deal about such attitudes from the many opinion polls we read about. We soon discover, however, that these beliefs and attitudes lack plausibility. They are arbitrary and not sufficiently anchored. And they lack the substance out of which plausible world views are created. Although in the modern world conviction is harder to sustain, it is our contention that, without the element of conviction, it is difficult to create a world we ourselves can value.

So why a book about martyrdom and the social construction of conviction? It is our thesis that culture and values are only plausible when there is the possibility of dying for them. Although convictions arouse our deepest suspicions and represent a great danger to the human race, we cannot construct worlds of meaning without them. These are the martyr's dilemmas, and they are the dilemmas we will address in the various portions of the book.

In the first chapter of Part I, we set the framework for our study, and present our definitions of the three basic elements in the ideal martyrological situation: the martyrological confrontation, the martyr's motive, and the martyrological narrative. We then present a brief synopsis of the main theories of conviction and a review of the martyrological literature leading towards a sociological theory of martyrdom.

Chapter Two traces the origins of classical martyrdom through a dynamic historical analysis of the martyr as a changing and interacting social type. From the period of Antiochan oppression over two thousand years ago, the development of the protomartyr and the martyr is traced in interaction with the zealot, the pro-Hellenist and the warrior athlete. This historical material sets the stage for our continuing sociological analysis.

In Part II, we turn the lens of our sociological analysis on each of the three basic components of classical martyrdom in order to trace within them those linkages which relate to conviction and its dilemmas.

Chapter Three presents our case for the impact of the martyrological confrontation and the martyr's conviction on the plausibility of culture and commitment. We claim that, in response to confrontation, martyrdom has a powerful impact on the early formation of groups, and on the validation and falsification of beliefs. The social purposes of the martyr are discussed and analyzed. The martyrdom of Jesus, which has had such a major impact on western civilization, is a subject in its own right, and it is alluded to particularly in this chapter.

A sociological analysis of the martyr's motive is the main subject of Chapter Four. The issues of the social validation of martyrdom and the limits of social control are raised, and the various elements involved in the sustaining of the martyr motivation are analyzed. A case study in which the prior psychological predisposition towards martyrdom is dominant is contrasted with those situations in which true believers are led to martyrdom through their identification with a powerful cause.

In our fifth chapter we present several examples of the manipulation of conviction through the fabrication of the martyr narrative. The secular use of the martyr narrative during the French Revolution is discussed, but the majority of the chapter is devoted to Goebbels and the fabrication of the Horst Wessel narrative in Nazi Germany. The various versions of the Horst Wessel narrative are presented in considerable detail in order to get a sense of the process and its incremental impact.

Finally, in the last chapter, we discuss the predicament of modern man with regard to conviction. It is a predicament which arises from the inclination to both value conviction because it is essential for the human spirit, and to fear it because it is so dangerous for the survival of humanity. This is the predicament with which the book began and it is our aim to shed some light on this issue. We believe that studying martyrdom and the way it is socially constructed offers some helpful insights in this connection.

Part One

CONVICTION AND THE STUDY
OF MARTYROLOGY

1

Towards a Sociological Theory of Martyrdom

The Martyrological Literature

The martyr has played a central role in western consciousness for hundreds of years. Over the centuries, the martyr's strength of conviction has been a source of fascination to martyrological researchers, and a voluminous body of literature with a genre of its own has been produced. Through primary accounts and through learned expositions we have access to vast quantities of information about the death of martyrs (e.g. Delehaye, 1927; Lieberman, 1939, Baron, 1957; Musurillo, 1972; Turner, 1974). In fact, the Catholic Bollandist Fathers, a dedicated Order of Priests, have focused their energies on the collection, editing and publication of martyrological narratives since 1613. One could thus hardly hope to deal with more than a fraction of the material collected on martyrs and their conviction.

In our pursuit of the social construction of conviction through the study of the martyr as a social type,[1] the extant martyrological

---

[1]Social type is a technical term in the sociological literature. Introduced by George Simmel it was elaborated on most recently by George Arditi, "Theory of Society" 16:565-591 (1987) in contrast to the notion of social role." ... the concept of social type implies a permanent connection between an individual and a structural condition ... in the concept of social type the person is perceived as the possessor of a character. This character is social in the sense that it originated because of structural arrangements of the society. The person is not an actor, someone 'who comes forward to play certain parts on the stage of society,' he or she is 'someone irretrievably within the play.' The character lives within the play, and the play comprises the essence of his or her reality. 'The actor leaves the stage; the character really may not do so. The actor belongs to the same world as the author, and participates in the making of a fiction; the character is in a closed world.' According to the concept of social types we live within one social reality, and this determines to a great extent what we are. The

literature has been our key source of material. We discovered from the outset that a certain methodological skepticism is in order while reading classical martyrologies. The stories do not represent accurate historical accounts in many cases, and frequently there is no external corroborating evidence which could verify that the events or persons depicted are historically factual.

We must, thus, assume that these stories provide for the most part only an accurate account of the author's imaginative world. It is a world, however, which does not lack sociological importance. If we can isolate the time and place in which the author lived, and, more importantly, if we can identify the author's social and political perspective, we can then begin to reconstruct his conceptual framework and the collective imagination of his society. In the sociological analysis of martyrdom, and the social construction of conviction, these perspectives, frameworks and imaginings are significant. When dealing with secondary texts, analysis must proceed with caution, focusing primarily on the world view of the author, rather than that of his or her protagonist.

Towards a Definition of Martyrdom

Since we have chosen the martyr as the ideal reflection of resolute conviction in a society, we now turn to the perplexing problem of definitions. Constructing a working definition of the martyr is complex. Every culture in classical antiquity as well as in modern times has a list of heroes which bear some resemblance to our intuitive conception of the martyr, i.e. anyone with sufficient conviction to be willing to suffer or die for a cause, and in any discussion on martyrdom one finds many "instant experts." However, after a moment's reflection, the matter is not so simple.

Most people would agree that Socrates, the Maccabean heroes, Eleazer, Hannah and her seven sons, Jesus, Ignatius of the Early Christian Church, and Joan of Arc are martyrs. Closer to our time, Rosa Luxemburg, Dietrich Bonhoeffer, Patrice Lamumba, Che Guevara,

---

behavior that derives from it is pervasive, permanent." p. 572. We perceive martyrs as a social type with a persistent character, located within a structured community of believers rather than as an actor who assures a social role with the characteristic detachment that accompanies the role concept. For the use of social type in the sense we are using c.f. Orin Klapp, *Symbolic Leaders* (Chicago, Aldine Publishing Co., 1964); *Heroes, Villains and Fools* (Englewood Cliffs, N.J., Prentice Hall, 1962); Stanley Cohen, *Folk Devils and Moral Panics, The Creating of Mods and Rockers* (London, Paladin Books, 1972); David Snow and Richard Mackaleck, "The Convert as a Social Type" in *Sociological Theory*, 1983, ed. Randall Collins (San Francisco, Jossey-Bass Publishers, 1983).

Malcolm X and Martin Luther King Jr. are martyrs in some sense of the term.

In contemplating this list, it is clear that not all are martyrs in the same sense. There are those whom one senses do not belong, but it is difficult to determine which are the missing characteristics. The term martyr, in spite of its clear etymological meaning of "witness," contains certain ambiguities in everyday usage. Rather than present an etymological discourse on the term martyr, (see Frend, 1966; Malone, 1959), we will now attempt, instead, to set a framework for our study.

Common usage dictates that there are three basic ways to become a martyr:

1. choosing to suffer or die rather than give up one's faith or principles.
2. being tortured or killed because of one's convictions
3. suffering great pain or misery for a long time.

There are, thus, three major factors that emerge from common usage i.e. choice, suffering and conviction. These three factors are not necessarily present in a given case, and there are several ambiguities which are generated by each factor that in turn require specification.

First, the term "martyr" encompasses people who are active, as well as some who are passive in the issues relating to their suffering and death. Some martyrs actively choose to suffer and die for their convictions, while others passively accept the suffering imposed on them.

Secondly, there are martyrs whose convictions are clearly stated and espoused. There are others, however, who are not particularly noted for their articulated convictions, but they are made to suffer in a painful or prolonged way.

The third ambiguity is related to the origins and the construction of each martyr. Why are some people who suffer for their convictions martyrized, while others are not? It is not at all clear who or what actually makes the martyr. Is it a matter of personal intention, dramatic circumstances, agonizing experiences or simply clever propaganda? Does the martyr primarily make him or herself? Is the martyr created by the persecutor and the oppression? In other words, are martyrs created through particular external circumstances, or through the unique force of their internal convictions?

All of these ambiguities are alluded to in George Bernard Shaw's clever depiction of Joan of Arc's treatment in history (Shaw, 1954). "Joan of Arc, a village girl...was born in 1412; burnt for heresy, witchcraft and sorcery in 1431; rehabilitated after a fashion in 1456;

designated Venerable in 1904; declared Blessed in 1908; and finally canonized in 1920. She is the most notable warrior-saint in the Christian Calendar, and the queerest fish among the eccentric worthies of the middle ages." In the light of common usage ambiguities, it is not at all clear just when we can say with some assurance that Joan of Arc first became a martyr. Was it in 1431, in 1456, 1904 or in 1920?

Since we do not claim to settle these difficulties in our presentation, we propose, for the purpose of our study of the social construction of conviction, a somewhat restrictive definition of martyrdom. In this book, the term "martyr" will refer to a social type located somewhere between the innocent hero and the suicidal zealot. The martyr will be seen as a member of a suppressed group who, when given the opportunity to renounce aspects of his or her group's code, willingly submits to suffering and death rather than forsake a conviction.

The Structural Framework of the Martyr as an Ideal Type

In ideal terms, martyrdom includes three basic elements; the martyrological confrontation, a structured situation in which the martyr confronts his or her persecutor; the martyr's motive - a disposition on the part of the martyr to self sacrifice for conviction; and the martyrological narrative - a literary tradition that immortalizes the martyr's story.

The Martyrological Confrontation

A martyrological event in the ideal sense, requires a confrontation between two types of individuals or groups. There is generally a dissenting, deviant, non-conforming person or group, with an alternative set of convictions, and a dominant powerful person or group willing to exercise its power. Martyrdom as an event is created out of the confrontation between the two.

From an examination of the classical sources, the components of an ideal martyrological confrontation include the following elements:

(a) A dissident individual is threatened with punishment if he or she persists in holding certain beliefs and convictions and behaving in ways that are proscribed by the ruling powers.

(b) The confrontation with the ruling powers, who persecute the dissident individual, takes place in a public setting.

(c) The individuals who are to undergo the agony of the test make a statement justifying their persistence in the proscribed belief or practice.

(d) The persecutor states his willingness to desist in applying punishment for non-conformity to established norms if the martyr will only recant and renounce his convictions.

(e) The martyr issues a statement of defiance, which affirms the preference of death to the betrayal of the espoused cause or principle.

(f) The established powers question the sanity or wisdom of the martyr-designate.

(g) The martyr rejects the services of mediators who attempt to blur the sharp differences between the victim and the persecutor(s).

(h) The martyr rejects all devices designed to achieve the ruse of symbolic betrayal of his cause and create the impression of his subordination to the persecutors.

(i) The martyr restates the purposes and convictions that justify the sacrifice of his life.

(j) The sufferer issues a profession of faith coupled with an expression of hope for his ultimate vindication.

(k) The martyr-designate is put to death.

As mentioned, not all martyrological confrontations include these elements, but in the framework of the martyr as an ideal type, each element plays a significant role.

The Martyr's Motive

Martyrs are typically persons who prefer to endure torture or death rather than forsake their values and convictions. However, from an examination of Jewish and early Christian traditions, (which are quite similar with regard to martyrdom, e.g. Lieberman, 1939; Baron, 1957), the ideal disposition for a martyr is not what one would expect. The unidimensional, untroubled espousal of a belief, and an uncompromising affirmation of a cause in the face of a threat to life, is not what one usually finds. Such perfect commitment would appear to be inhuman.

What emerges from the historical evidence is that the most impressive of the martyrs are hesitating human beings who are subject to doubt. Their martyrological circumstances have been thrust upon them; their convictions grow and solidify through trials and tribulations. The martyr is typically willing to engage in second thoughts about going through with the whole affair. What emerges is that the most effective motive in practice is not a steadfast, uncompromising, free choice of a principled belief. The martyr's motive, if it is to be believable and emulatable, (and both these qualities constitute its efficacy), is usually somewhat mixed in the sense which we have sketched out.

The Martyrological Narrative

Most of the actual sacrifices for a cause are never transformed into martyrdoms. What is required is that a martyrologist be around to chronicle those raw occurrences into *events* of social significance. It is then necessary to fashion the events so they relate a story.

Martyrdom becomes influential through the narratives that celebrate it. These narratives determine the symbolic fate of the martyr and his or her posthumous immortality. It is the viability of the narrative's transmission which becomes the measure of the martyr's significance.

Like all stories, the martyr's narrative is shaped according to the oral and literary traditions of the culture within which it circulates. If it circulates within a cultural tradition that venerates the tragic form, it too will be touched and influenced by the tragic. (Henn, 1966; Kaufmann, 1969; Steiner, 1961) If, for example, the tradition is a liturgical one, the martyrology will bear the marks of liturgical conventions. (Delehaye, 1927).

An important point to bear in mind is that the narrative does not necessarily have to be formulated at the time of the martyr's death, nor even by those who were alive at that time. Some of the most successful narratives were created by martyrologists who were not witnesses to the martyrological happenings (e.g. Eusebius and Foxe). In fact some of the most noteworthy narratives have been created out of the pure imagination of the martyrologist.

The three components outlined above are vividly illustrated in the ideal images of such classical martyrs as the Maccabeans – Hannah and Eleazer – Jesus, and the canonized version of Joan of Arc. In these instances, the martyr's motive is clear and noble, the dramatic confrontation is fully played out in the public arena, and there are authorized versions of the hero's death.

There are, however, cases in which one or two of the central martyrological components are missing. As we shall see in the case of Horst Wessel, the Nazi party activist killed in a brawl, and presented in full elsewhere in this book, there are even instances of "fabricated martyrs." Wessel had neither a principled motive, nor an appropriate confrontation with a persecutor, but he did have the benefit of a brilliant martyrological narrative that was sold by Joseph Goebbels to a gullible public.

The Sacco and Vanzetti case is also interesting. One clearly perceives here a dramatic confrontation and an abundance of rich martyrological narratives created by the media. Yet, it is far from clear that the "martyrs" themselves had any idea what conviction they were dying for. Dietrich Bonhoeffer, the minister executed by Nazis far from the public view, was denied a public display of his heroic conviction. Yet, Bonhoeffer clearly possessed the martyrological motive, and his death evoked a spate of martyrological narratives.

Finally, there are all those individuals like Bernard Shaw's character, Spintho, an early Christian, who loses heart and forsakes his comrades' penchant for martyrdom. He runs out the wrong door of the coliseum in an effort to escape, and to his great shock finds himself in the arena with a hungry lion. Spintho meets a "Martyr's end" - and is celebrated in spite of himself. He remains an everlasting witness to the importance of both hungry lions and good story tellers when it comes to the creation of martyrs. Spintho's story is a powerful example of the paradoxes involved in the social construction of conviction.

Why People Die for Their Convictions:
Competing Theories of Martyrdom

There are many theories of martyrdom which attempt to explain why people die for their convictions. Although most are incisive and essentially correct in their interpretations, none of them encompass the entire phenomenon of martyrdom. In this book we have chosen to discuss in depth three of the extant theories; The psychologistic theory, and two sociological theories; Riddle's theory of social control (Riddle, 1931), and Turner's theory of cultural heritage (Turner, 1974). We will now turn to a brief consideration of the competing theories of martyrdom.

The Tyrannical Persecutor Theory

Classical martyrdom is often accompanied by a dramatic confrontation between a ruler with visions of his own divinity and a group with deviant convictions. According to this theory, martyrdom and self sacrifice flourish when rulers make megalomaniacal demands for displays of total loyalty from their subjects. These demands produce anger and counter-displays of loyalty to convictions which are forbidden. It is the centrality of the villain as tyrannical persecutor which is used to explain the role that Antiochus, Caligula, Hadrian, Decius and Diocletian played in the development of Jewish Hellenistic and Early Christian martyrdom. (Tcherikover, 1959)

Although the truth of this theory is clear, in our opinion the view that martyrdom is the result of a cruel persecutor is too narrow. It overlooks the great variety of situations in which the phenomenon of martyrdom occurs without such tyrannical persecution.

The Theory of Situation as Cause

According to this theory, martyrdom is the result of ordinary people being pushed beyond a certain critical threshold within the context of a public confrontation. It is the predictable outcome of public confrontations between the powerful who feel threatened and the weak who have principles. The contrast between the position of the weak and the powerful is ever present. However, it is only when public confrontations offer the weak no reasonable exit from their principles and compliance is publicly forced, that the weak have no choice but to martyr themselves.

A variation of this approach is the Theory of Honor (Berger 1970). Based on a historical description of the importance of honor in groups, the emphasis in this theory is on the situation of social degradation. When such a point is reached, people are willing to sacrifice their lives. Preservation of one's honor and self respect become the highest priorities of all.

Under ordinary conditions, according to both these theories, the weak have no need to martyr themselves for their principles. They can attempt to strengthen their position through less dramatic means. However, when they are pushed beyond a certain point, martyrdom becomes the only reasonable tactical response to the situation. The role of the martyr as a passive actor responding to unreasonable circumstances is an accurate reflection of some, but not all martyrological situations.

The Human Nature Theory

This theory has many variations. The fundamental idea is that not the persecutor, not the convictions, and not the situation, but something in human nature is the cause of martyrdom. It may be due to an altruistic gene (Wilson, 1975,1978), a masochistic need (Menninerg, 1938), an undeniable existential aspiration, an obsession with death (Byman, 1974), the need for transcendence (Lipton, 1967), the inevitability of victimhood (Burke, 1965), or the need to dramatize values.

Due to the universality of the phenomenon, we are respectful of the claims made about human nature and martyrdom. However, we remain both skeptical and critical of this view as an inclusive explanation. Once again, we believe this view to be too general to encompass the specificity of the phenomenon, with its many historical variations.

The Theory of Group Predisposition

In this explanation martyrdom is viewed not as a universal phenomenon but as the inclination of certain groups. Its causes are historically conditioned. The groups most frequently studied during the past few decades have been the Jews, Christians, Shiite Moslems, Buddhists, segments of the Black Community in America, and Women (Stein, 1978; Valentine, 192; Lefkowitz, 1976). Most writers within this tradition attribute the predisposition towards martyrdom to cultural and psychological factors. A particularly dominant theme in this approach is the "need for failure," and the programming of this need into the culture and into the repertoire of acceptable group behavior.

While this explanation is useful in some cases, seeing martyrdom as the predisposition of only certain groups overlooks the fact that it is virtually universal.

The Theory of Narration

According to this theory, martyrdom is essentially a story; a structured transmission of happenings within a body of oral and written traditions. Ultimately, the text is the most important factor in martyrdom. The historical veracity of the events recorded is a secondary issue. Once they are embodied in a text, the fact that they did not occur does not detract from their persuasive power. To understand martyrdom is essentially to understand a story, and to explain it one must grapple with the text.

We have been much influenced by those who view martyrdom as essentially a narrative, and we relate to this issue both in the section on Narratives and in the chapter on Manipulation of Conviction.

The Theory of Group Imitation and Competition

According to this theory, martyrdom as a cultural tradition is diffused through imitation and competition among groups. To elaborate this theory, the period studied in greatest depth is the Middle Ages (Spiegel, 1967).

Once again, although the groups studied verify aspects of this theory, explaining the phenomenon of martyrdom as a kind of parochial imitation of other groups' behavior does not account for its universality among known cultures and groups.

The Theory of Psychological Aberration

The emphasis in this explanation of martyrdom is on masochistic tendencies, self destructive inclinations, group frenzy and seizure by irrational forces.

Although useful in understanding the predisposition of some martyrs toward martyrdom, we believe that these widely accepted psychological explanations are unnecessarily reductionistic. The psychological approach has had a powerful impact on western consciousness during the past several decades, and, from our point of view, these psychological explanations have successfully inhibited the creation of more inclusive, sociologically oriented explanations. (Reik, 1976; Menninger, 1938; Masaryk, 1970)

The Theory of the Cultural Heritage

Martyrdom, according to this theory, is the result of a received tradition. Since this approach will be discussed in detail throughout the book, we will here simply indicate that the emphasis in this theory is on the process in which martyrdom becomes embedded in the culture via religion, rituals, popular folk beliefs, literature and symbols.

We believe that there is great value in regarding martyrdom as a developing process of incorporating certain key ideas relating to sacrifice and atonement into the cultural heritage of a people, and we will be reflecting on this theory in various portions of our book. (Turner, 1974)

The Theory of Social Control

It is the role that the social forces play in the creation of martyrdom which is essentially the subject of this book. During the 1920's and 1930's the concept of social control implied the capacities of a group to control the loyalty of its members and to preserve their commitment (Janowitz, 1975). We have found this early perspective on social control, which formed the theoretical framework for Riddle's (1931) study of martyrdom, helpful and it has guided a good deal of our thinking. Over the years, the meaning of the term social control has changed, and in the 1950's and 1960's it implied the capacity of the group to exercise power over individuals and to coerce them towards adherence to group norms. The early usage of the term has been more useful in our study.

We have chosen to stress the social factors that contribute to martyrdom, and they form the theme which runs throughout our analysis. We should, however, point out that arguments and proofs from many other disciplines have been used to bolster our claims.

In summary, although the list we have presented is not all inclusive, we believe that all the important theories of martyrdom have been noted. As we have stated, we believe that some of the theories briefly presented are insightful but not sufficiently inclusive, while others we believe to lead in the wrong direction. Those which we have found useful have been included in the various sections of our analysis.

In this chapter we have thus far attempted to set the framework for our study of conviction and martyrdom through defining the martyrological context i.e. the confrontation, the motive and the narrative, and through the presentation of various theoretical approaches to the study of martyrdom. We will now systematically review various sociological treatments of martyrdom as a phenomenon and of the martyr as a social type.

Towards a Sociological Theory of Martyrdom

As observers of human group behavior, sociologists have been interested in martyrs since the birth of sociology. The sacrifice of the self for a social cause is a matter of great strategic importance for the social group, and martyrs can be found in every form of social aggregation including civilizations, religions, societies, nations, social movements, small groups and families.

For the most part, however, rather than studying martyrdom as a subject in its own right, sociologists have subsumed their interest in martyrs under some other category of concern. There are many examples of this; Durkheim studied some of the early Christian martyrs as examples of altruistic suicide (1951); Weber treated the martyrdom of 2nd Isaiah in the context of the problem of theodicy; Merton's brief but incisive discussion of the martyr was an example of the historically significant nonconformist (1965); Mill's analysis of the martyr was an example of the institutional selection of persons for social roles and for a "vocabulary of motives" (1963); Bellah emphasized the importance of martyrs for the legitimation of civil religion (1985) and Toth considered the martyr as a catalyst in the creation of social movements (1972).

The two major exceptions to this secondary treatment of the martyr have been Riddle's (1931) sociological analysis of early Christian Martyrs and Klapp's rather extensive discussions of martyrdom in his works (1954, 1958, 1974). There is some truth in the social historian, Kelley's complaint, however: "In all the massive literature on martyrs I find no useful studies ... from a socio-historical point of view" (1973). Although this blanket and global dismissal of the work done so far is extreme, in our view the subject of the martyr is in need of a sociological analysis which is not oblique or intermittent, but which is the result of the same measure of intellectual commitment as is devoted to the study of other social types.

On the other hand, in allied social science disciplines, this kind of intellectual commitment has been forthcoming. The martyr and martyr-like behavior has been the central focus of a good deal of empirical and historical research in social psychology, psychology, cultural anthropology and psycho-history. Since there is considerable overlap between a proposed sociological treatment of the martyr and the interests, concepts and central focus of studies in these allied fields, we propose to now consider them. The key areas which have been studied are the following:

The Martyr Mother and Intra-Psychic Pathology

Those studies which concentrate on the causes and the effects of martyr-like behavior generally define such behavior as a pathological manifestation of intra psychic processes. The behavior defined as martyr-like includes: "subtle and devious tactics of self sacrifice for the purpose of inducing and inferring guilt in others, a kind of impotent, futile, hopeless victimization of self and others" (Heilbrun, 1972), The martyr mother and her damaged offspring, as well as the physically and psychologically disabled, are the key target groups in these studies.

Martyr mother studies have dealt with such topics as: the contribution of the martyr mother to the incidence of schizophrenia in her children (Wolman, 1969; Heilbrun, 1972; and Loney, 1973), the adoption of the martyr mother role as a response to the social pathology of the father (Garrett, 1975), The influence of early childhood socialization on the development of the martyr mother role (Mitchell, 1973), the incapacity of the martyr mother to work outside the home (Wagenheim, 1972), or the role adopted by women in cases of prolonged father absence (Marsella, 1974).

One of the noteworthy aspects of these martyr mother studies is their universal emphasis on the negative effects produced by the woman who behaves in a martyr-like way. Nowhere, to our knowledge, has there been any consideration of the possible good which might have come from the martyr mother, and this should arouse some suspicion as to the scientific objectivity of the studies. Can it be true that no good at all can come from the "Yiddishe Mama" and her ethnic counterparts?

In all these studies, there is a tendency to regard the martyr mother as a toxic causal agent who has a deleterious effect on everyone and everything she comes into contact with. She is responsible for lesbianism in daughters, homosexuality in sons, and her martyr-like behavior is significantly correlated with rapists, incest offenders, alcoholics, and certain types of schizophrenic disorders, e.g. Loney (1973). With this total absence of positive traits, one cannot help wondering if the martyr-mother, instead of only martyring herself, is not being martyred by her very bright and verbally gifted children.

One of the major difficulties in these studies is that the behavior of the martyr mother is neither specified nor differentiated from the behavior of other mothers. It is assumed that everyone knows what a martyr mother is like, and no specific behaviors are described. There are many questions which remain unanswered; for instance, who or what does the martyr mother sacrifice? Is it herself, her children, her husband, her opportunities, her health, her life, or perhaps all or part of these.

Perhaps the behavior of the martyr mother is the result of free choice, not of constraint? And what is the cause she sacrifices herself for? Is it her own sense of personal rectitude, or does she sacrifice herself for her children, for her husband, for the ideal conception of her role? With regard to this alleged sacrifice, is it real or only impression management? What is the degree of personal commitment to the role? The studies we have mentioned deal only peripherally with questions such as these.

In our view, one of the reasons the martyr mother studies do not deal with these questions is because the martyr per se as a social type is generally not well understood. For example, as we shall see in Chapter Two, it would be worthwhile for those interested in the martyr mother to consider the historical sources where martyr mothers have been memorialized. Even a cursory examination of these sources would reveal the wide range of behaviors characteristic of the classical martyr mothers. The martyr mother Hannah, for instance, was willing to see her seven sons martyred for a conviction she herself held, while Perpetua was willing to sacrifice herself as a martyr although her infant son was deprived of a mother as a result.

There is a significant difference between the martyr mother who participates in the destruction of her children, and the mother who is destroyed together with her children (Foxe 1583); the mother who is martyred by her husband and children and the one who is the agent of her own real or imagined persecution. The uncritical, undefined use of the term martyr mother blurs and homogenizes all differential nuances.

The Physically and Psychologically Disabled

Martyr-like behavior has been studied as a counterproductive means for obtaining love (Lubin 1959); as a parental reaction to the retardation of children (Gardner, 1978); as a formidable obstacle to successful psychotherapy (Thompson, 1974); as a correlate to psychosomatic illness; and as a self destructive syndrome (Menninger, 1938). These studies are unanimous in the conclusion that martyrdom is essentially pathological behavior with negative antecedents and harmful consequences.

Martyr-like Behavior in Small Group Interaction

Within the context of game theory martyrdom has been operationalized as "cooperation to one's own detriment according to someone else's standards" or a "kind of super cooperation to the detriment of one's own interests" (Braver, 1975). Unlike the studies of intra-psychic pathology, in the field of small group interaction, martyr-like behavior can lead to such positive outcomes as more cooperative strategies from opponents (O'Grady, 1970), or to a higher degree of cooperation from future opponents who have watched the martyr-like behavior (Braver, 1975). Martyr-like behavior has been conceptualized as one of the four archetypal strategies in competition (Rappaport, 1967).

Apparently within the context of small group interaction, martyr-like behavior on the part of a group member is less destructive than within the context of a family. Although this difference has never been studied, the consensus is that there is an unstated but powerfully present equity norm in small groups. This norm becomes activated when one of the members engages in martyr-like behavior, and it leads to higher levels of cooperation between competitors for scarce resources.

Martyrs, Institutions and Social Movements

The contribution of martyrdom to the legitimation of controversial causes is the major focus of an interesting and valuable group of studies. Although many of these studies rely quite heavily on psychologistic explanations, they suggest a starting point for a more analytically oriented approach to the sociology of martyrdom.

In a methodologically meticulous study, Byman (1974) has analyzed the contribution of the Marian martyrs to the establishment of the English Church. He was interested in those biographical factors which predisposed the martyr towards self sacrifice. In his study, through an analysis of diaries and the contemporary accounts of observers, Byman manages to reveal the inner life and personal circumstances of the martyrs. Through his documentation, he demonstrates the interface between personal biographical defeats and traumas and the disposition towards martyrdom.

According to Byman, frustration in love, humiliation in business, crushed ambitions and unjust accusations all led to the committing of offenses which were the prelude to martyrdom. Byman's analysis rests heavily on the proposition that private troubles and traumas are the primary contexts within which martyrological issues arise. Byman tends to discount the announced motive which the martyr proclaims, and his research could thus be primarily classified as psychological. However, his studies are sociologically valuable because he does manage to depict those intervening social circumstances which contribute, together with a psychological predisposition, toward the creation of conditions for martyrdom. Some of those intervening social circumstances are: the existence of a religious oriented culture; a theology of an after-life; and a very punishing super-ordinate authority.

If Byman's research suffers from a surfeit of psychologistic explanation, then Methvin's study of the process whereby martyrs are manufactured in order to elicit support for radical causes has precisely the opposite defect. Methvin (1970) has an axe to grind. He is interested in revealing how the making of martyrs is a tactic in the radicalization of innocent and gullible crowds. The internal disposition of martyrs is of less interest to him, although he does give us some insight into the inner lives of the Buddhist priests who cremated themselves. He regards them primarily as duped innocents.

Methvin is less interested in martyrs than in those that create them - in the martyrizers. His point is that causes need martyrs and if none are available then they must be manufactured. His study is a documentation of this process of manufacture, of "providing the crowd with a martyr." According to Methvin, fellow party members are presented as martyrs to the party cause even after they have been intentionally murdered by party adherents. Through their fabricated martyrdom, as we shall see in Chapter Five, their cause is dramatized and support is elicited. While Methvin's documentation is sparse and for the most part unconvincing, his points are suggestive and, as we shall see in the case of Nazi Germany and the legend of Horst Wessel, they must be taken into account in any sociological account of martyrdom.

Vree's study of the Berrigan brothers during the Vietnamese war (1975) is an analysis of the social significance of martyrdom and of its social limitations. Vree evaluated the efficacy of the martyr symbol in the political behavior of the Berrigan brothers and found that enormous feelings of guilt were aroused by their sacrifice. This guilt was then manipulated in order to elicit support for their cause.

In addition, the martyrological sacrifice with its imagery of purification, death and rebirth gives the martyr, in his own eyes and in those of sympathetic bystanders, a moral warrant to judge others. The purification that results from "stripping oneself clear" seems to provide the martyr with a sense of self righteousness that makes it legitimate in the eyes of observers for him or her to judge others. By comparison to the purity of the martyr-self, others are found to be morally wanting.

Vree is essentially arguing that the martyrological sacrifice brings into being a radicalizing transvaluation of morality. According to Vree, the martyr is dangerous to the democratic process which is based on a rational give and take and on a process of compromise. The martyr is incapable of making compromises since his or her world is filled with radical convictions, a disdain for conventional morality, and a critique of everything that does not measure up to the purity of his own motive. The importance of life is devaluated and there is no respect for majority opinion.

Wood, Pilsuk and Uren's research (1973) provides useful clues to the impact of martyr-behavior on its observers. Their research was done in the context of Prisoner Dilemma games and it shows that, contrary to most prevalent theories, martyr behavior does not arouse guilt. It is shame, not guilt, that such behavior arouses. In their definition, guilt is related to the superego and past actions, while shame is related to the ego ideal and future actions. Using psychological tests which distinguish between guilt and shame, they found that shame is related to high self esteem and to a higher valuation of the martyr.

Individuals with high self-esteem can accept the non-conformity of the martyr without feelings of personal threat. Their sense of self worth is based on inner standards of judgement which are not threatened by non conformity. People with low self-esteem, on the other hand, do not value the martyr's behavior because the martyr is challenging standards of evaluation which are external to them.

In their research, Wood, Pilsuk and Uren did not find that the tolerance for ambiguity as a personality trait was related to evaluating the martyr's behavior. Their assumption had been that those who had difficulty with uncertainty would tend to value martyrdom negatively, since the outcome of the martyrological situation is unclear once the action sequence begins. They found that this was not the case. It is the certainty of the martyr's conviction which makes its mark on the observers, and which evokes admiration and emulation. Not guilt or uncertainty determine the acceptance or rejection of the martyr, but rather the values of the martyr as a guide for possible future action. It is an "aspiration for" rather than a "recoiling from" that is determinative in the reactions of audiences.

An interesting related finding was that the martyr's sacrifice elicits widespread adoption of the principle behind the behavior, but not of the self-sacrifice itself. Cooperative behavior among the observers of the self sacrifice was greater than among non-observers. The authors speculate that had they managed to arrange for feedback to their subjects on the emulation of the martyr's behavior, the impact may have been even greater.

It is difficult to generalize from their research to the actual historical instances of martyrdom, but some important issues are raised. In situations where the martyr's principles are valued, it is not unreasonable to assume that the martyr's behavior might be imitated under certain conditions. There does indeed seem to be a contagion effect of martyrdom in some historical instances, so that the more martyrs there were, the more there continued to be.

In their ethnographic study of the Black Panther movement, the Valentines (1972) are concerned with the fact that martyrdom is used as a discrediting label against the Black Panthers. Those Afro-Americans who sacrificed their lives for group social advancement were not celebrated as martyrs for the cause, but were regarded as exhibitionists caught up with a mania for suicide. The Valentine research alerts us to the fact that martyrdom can be used as a discrediting term when consciously linked to an unreasonable craving for suicide. This kind of discrediting is a variation of the pathological theme in martyrological research.

In the Panther's case the method of discrediting involves the use of data from the social sciences. Statistics are first presented to demonstrate that the rate of suicide among blacks is higher than other groups. Evidence is then brought to show that black revolutionaries "invite death at the hands of others." Through the use of "defiant and provocative rhetoric" these revolutionaries are depicted as "victims of precipitated homicide." According to the Valentines, these depictions serve the interests of "the man," and justify a policy of extermination. The professed ideology of the Black Panther leaders is investigated by the Valentines in order to show how their "revolutionary suicide" is, in truth, not suicide, but a refusal to die in the ghetto. Life in the ghetto is viewed as the "reactionary suicide" of submission to oppression.

While their treatment of the subject can hardly be regarded as dispassionate they nonetheless alert us to some moral dimensions of the use of martyrdom. The main issue that emerges from the Valentine's analysis is that martyrdom can be a discrediting term if linked to pathological psychologistic claims by the observer. This appears to be the case in the Western evaluation of Shiite behavior. In short, there is no guarantee that sympathy will be elicited when a person is regarded as a martyr. "Martyr" can be used as a pejorative term. The Valentines have helped us to understand the circumstances in which this stigmatization takes place.

Martyrdom is related to Weber's concept of charisma in a study by Toth (1972). Toth distinguishes between the charisma of the outer call, and that of the inner consolidation. The outer call represents the breaking out of established molds of social structure with a new message, while the inner consolidation involves the capacity to integrate a new charismatic message in a structure capable of bearing it. There is a similarity between Toth's interpretation and that of Nisbit (1970), but with Toth, charisma is embodied in pairs of people whose actions complement one another.

The charismatics of the outer call such as Jesus, Joseph Smith, Lenin, Martin Luther King, Jr. and Che Guevera, require charismatics of the inner consolidation such as Paul, B. Young, Stalin, Abernathy and Castro, in order to succeed. We need not concern ourselves here with whether this is a legitimate usage of the term charisma or not. What is interesting is that in many of these situations of cooperation between two leaders it is the martyrdom of the first that helps the consolidating follower to achieve integration of the social movement. Toth alerts us to the fact that it is not enough for a social movement to have a martyr. And Smith (1974) reminds us that the Movement without a martyr is impoverished; but there must also be a leader left alive after the martyrdom to elicit involvement and engage in the activity of group formation.

The Myth of the Martyr in Social Conflict

While many historians, theologians and poets have demonstrated the power of the martyr myth in situations of social conflict, Victor Turner (1974) has brought these insights together in a masterful historical treatment of martyrs. Turner is interested in martyrdom as a process as well as an event. He explores: 1. The power of the martyr myth to delegitimize superordinate power; 2. The power of the martyr myth to give revolutionary causes memorable and dramatic statements; and 3. The ability of the martyr myth to tap into what he calls a root paradigm, by calling forth deeply buried, but powerfully felt, cultural sentiments. These sentiments, when mobilized by martyrdom, provide legitimacy and significance to the cause espoused.

In his treatment of Thomas Becket and Hidalgo, Turner highlights the potency of the martyr myth in situations of social conflict. He is interested in the unfolding of the martyrological event and in describing the process that made Becket and Hidalgo martyrs. He describes how they used the cultural traditions at their disposal to enhance their own credibility. What emerges from this powerful analysis is an understanding of how Becket and Hidalgo undermined the secular power through their use of martyrological traditions embedded in the cultures of which they were a part.

Some Preliminary Questions and Conclusions

From our review of the martyrological literature in the social sciences, it is clear that the martyr seems to deeply touch some basic human need. There are correspondingly strong responses to martyrdom on the biological, psychic, social and cultural levels. The source of this potency, however, is not at all clear. Are these responses rooted in the psychic makeup of the individual? Is the universal presence of martyr-like behavior connected to some biologically determined altruistic process? Is it related to some social need necessary for the functioning of the group? Is martyrdom deeply encoded in cultural traditions? Is it the result of some widespread need for the dramatization of human purposes? Or is martyrdom a name given to disparate things that are only loosely connected? Is it merely a historically limited expression of human behavior from which no broad generalizations can be made regarding psychic process, social interaction or cultural transmission?

Whatever our questions concerning martyrdom, one thing cannot be doubted; martyrdom has an impact both in the world around us ... and for most of recorded historical time.

Like all symbols, martyrdom condenses many meanings into one act. Martyrdom connotes purity of motive, conviction, commitment, selfless sacrifice, surety of reward beyond this life, courage in the face of agony, dramatic gesture, sincerity and so on. As with many symbols some of the associations are contradictory.

It is, however, precisely this tension which creates the power of its suggestiveness as a symbol. As we in the western world have experienced with the spread of Christianity, martyrdom has strong evocative potential not only for the actual spectators but for those who can be drawn into its symbolic world of death and hope; expiation and guilt; exemplary action and evil; naivete and concrete interests; happiness and suffering. These tightly condensed meanings are all the more powerful because of their potential capacity to be circulated in a wide variety of settings and historical circumstances.

The Social Construction of the Martyrological Sacrifice

The martyrological sacrifice is not only the action of an individual martyr, with his or her compelling or particular motivation. It is also a social construction in which many kinds of social actors participate. One becomes a martyr not only by doing things but also having things done to one within a social context, particularly within a situation of confrontation between a persecutor and a representative of an unacceptable conviction. It is an act that is then proclaimed to have happened, and is ultimately socially legitimized and celebrated in a narrative.   In addition, the evaluation of the martyrological sacrifice is not necessarily related to immediately apparent interests. One of the paradoxical aspects of the martyrological sacrifice is that those who come in contact with the martyr do not necessarily act in accordance with their own interests. Those who interact with the martyr feel bound by some principle of restorative equity to right the wrongs that have been perpetrated. The martyr's sacrifice arouses new and powerful feelings that have an unsettling effect on prior moral commitments and conceptions of self interest. Martyrdom appears to encourage the cooperation of antagonists, to mute the competition among rivals and to arouse empathy on the part of persecutors.

The martyrological sacrifice can be seen as a fundamental conflict strategy which emerges under specific historical circumstances. It does not just happen at any time, but is related to the origins of social movements and to moments of social crisis.

The Context of Martyrological Evaluation
and Psychologistic Perceptions

The context in which martyrdom occurs would appear to be an important aspect of its evaluation. Within the family, martyrdom tends to be negatively valued, especially by "emotionally involved" audiences. The forces unleashed by the martyrological sacrifice are apparently too powerful to be contained within the narrow confines of family life.

At present, the most widespread conception of the martyrological sacrifice is based on a psychologistic perception of the martyr's motive. According to this prevalent view, the most important determinative forces in martyrdom are the intrapsychic impulses, compulsions, and drives which impel the martyr to his or her sacrificial action. These drives are judged to be pathological.

We are interested in redressing this imbalance in perception. Social circumstances and cultural patterns are, in our view, determinants, but, lately, when they are not ignored or dismissed, they are for the most part regarded as derivative. As we have stated, we believe that this view of martyrdom is too narrow, and that the broader sociological perspective has much to add to our understanding of this important link between conviction and social norms.

These then are the major conclusions about martyrdom which emerge from our literature review. While none of them are terribly earth-shattering in their originality or insight, they do furnish us with some starting points in our pursuit of a sociological theory of martyrdom. In order to further this pursuit of the social construction of conviction, we will now turn to the classical sources of the martyr as a social type.

2

Conviction and Social Types: The Origins of Classical Martyrdom

Convictions are held by communities as well as by individuals. In order to understand why people are willing to die for their convictions we need to understand something about human communities and the way in which these communities recognize and support convictions among their members. It is our thesis that the western version of martyrdom as an expression of conviction was the result of a gradual historical process which took place during a particular period and under a particular set of circumstances. In this chapter we propose to trace this process in order to analyze the historical development of the martyr as a social type.

The Analysis of Social Types

Before we plunge into our search for the roots of Classical martyrdom, let us examine the sociological framework in which this analysis takes place, i.e. an analysis of the social type. Sociologists have long relied on social types as a professional tool in their study of societies. The most notable examples of such social types are: The Stranger (Simmel, 1950); The Marginal Man (Park, 1928); The Fool (Klapp, 1949); and the Political Eunuch (Coser, 1974). While the exact meaning of the term "social type" varies in these works, the term generally refers to some salient characteristics and role behavior of individuals with distinct positions in society (Coser, 1980).

There is some dispute in the sociological literature as to the precise difference between a social type and a social role. Social types, such as the one immortalized by Simmel, are generally viewed as less fluid and more static, seemingly frozen in prose. They attain quasi-literary immortality and do not seem to change very radically over time. Rarely do they lead to anything beyond themselves. The qualities in these social types which have been abstracted are reified and deemed relevant for most times and most social contexts. In our view, in this kind of an analysis the social type seems unnecessarily abstracted and unlinked to the historical context.

There have been a few recent and welcome exceptions in the sociological literature to this idealized depiction of social types (Coser, 1974; Griswold, 1983; Smith, 1974). In their analyses of social types they attempt to make a linkage between a social type and some social process. For example, Smith examines the Dandy as an instance of entrepreneurship in a situation where social structure is undergoing decay.

In short, the issue of the origin, development and dynamic changing nature of the social type has not been dealt with sufficiently in the sociological literature. Those who have enthusiastically taken up the challenge have been historians, philosophers and literary critics, (such as Camus), but their perspective does not generally include sociological concerns.

These issues are of concern to us in our study of martyrdom as a recognized expression of commitment to conviction. We have discovered that, over the centuries, the martyr as a social type has been far from a static entity, and has interacted significantly with the specific social context of the period.

In our analysis, our objective is to map out the social conditions and the structures of group consciousness which first lent plausibility to the emergence of the martyr figure. This type of analysis has not yet been attempted, to the best of our knowledge.[1] The great advantage of this perspective is that the martyr can be seen as more than a saint or a psychotic. It enables us to delve into the voluminous martyrdom literature without the value-laden devotion which views martyrs as sacred heroes, or the psychological perspective which ultimately reduces martyrs to masochistic exhibitionists. Although both these genres have value, they do not tell the entire story.

We, thus, propose to anchor our analysis of the martyr as a social type in two central assumptions:

---

[1]*Aside* from the work by Klapp, Smith and Griswold, there are some interesting treatments of social types and their connection with social structure: McIntyre, *After Virtue,* has a brief but very insightful treatment of one social type (the public school teacher in England) and the connection with the social structure. Green, *Dreams of Adventure, Deeds of Empire,* has done the same for the literary social type of Robinson Crusoe; Peter Berger has used Don Quixote as a model of the social type of the modern "individual."

1. Social Types function within specific social contexts. In order to understand the social type, the social context must be described. It is the social context which gives plausibility to the ideas and conceptions that provide meanings for the social type.[2] Reciprocally, an analysis of the social type provides a key to an understanding of the social context.

2. Social types are not static entities. Any attempt to understand them should include their origins, and their ongoing transformations. The tension and mutual interplay between the social type and the historically changing context is essential for an analysis which is valid.[3]

It is our contention that any future theory of social types must deal with these two elemental, but frequently overlooked assumptions. As we shall see in our study of the martyr, by including them, the analysis of social types can become a more powerful method of understanding social groups.

The Roots of Western Martyrdom[4]

Martyrdom, along with many other components of western civilization, first entered the arena of western consciousness during the ancient encounter between Greek and Israelite culture. In the first section of our analysis, we will demonstrate that an embryonic form of martyrdom, which we call "protomartyrdom" was originally developed by the Israelites in response to the religious persecution of Antiochus Epiphanes, 167-175 B.C.E.

Within the scholarly literature, the origin of the martyr is shrouded in confusion and controversy. Some accounts from within the theological framework trace the roots of martyrdom back to the story of Cain and Abel, while others begin with Jesus and Saint Stephen. The more value-neutral historians tend to fall into three camps. There are those who argue that the idea of martyrdom was first developed in the Greek hero cults. Others maintain that it was first conceived in the religious-nationalist culture of pre-Christian Palestine. Finally, there are those who claim that the concept originally crystallized in the

---

[2]c.f. Berger and Luckmann, *The Social Construction of Reality* (1967), for an elaboration of the notion of plausibility structures.

[3]Albert Camus has a historically sensitive treatment of the idea of the *Rebel* (1956) as a social type.

[4]The arguments to be found in our analysis lean heavily on three principal sources. The first is the work of W.H.C. Frend (1967) which traces the roots of Christian martyrdom back to the Jewish traditions. The second is that of W.E. Nickelsburg (1981) which offers a thorough analysis of the texts produced by Jews responding to the Antiochan persecution. Finally, our analysis of the Greek influences on the concept of martyrdom in *Fourth Maccabees* relies on the work of Moses Hadas (1953).

culture of Hellenistic Jews living on the periphery of ancient
Palestine.[5]

We will argue that the truth lies somewhere between these three
divergent viewpoints. Our claim is that in the early second century
B.C., the religious-nationalist culture of Judaea produced an idea
which approximates our conception of classical martyrdom. This
protomartyrdom concept was later combined with certain elements of
Greek-Hellenistic culture. It was in the combination of Greek and
Hebrew ideas that the first known accounts of classical martyrdom
were produced. In order to substantiate this thesis, we will now provide
some historical background concerning the Antiochan persecution.

The Historical Background of Protomartyrdom

In the year 175 B.C.E. Antiochus Epiphanes succeeded his brother,
Seleucid, to the throne of the Seleucid Empire. The Seleucid kingdom
was a component of the vast empire created originally by the conquests
of Alexander the Great. At the time of Antiochus' ascent to the throne,
the Seleucids controlled large territories in Syro-Palestine, Asia Minor
and Trans-Jordan. This area, which was ruled from Antioch, included
the tiny province known as "Judaea."

Judaea was primarily inhabited by Israelites living around
Jerusalem who worshipped the god Yahweh. Their daily lives were
governed by the code of Moses, a set of normative beliefs and practices
revealed by Yahweh at Sinai. The Mosaic Law provided the Israelites
with a strong sense of national identity as well as a distinctive
religious world view. Their religious-national culture evolved around a
cultic Temple in Jerusalem, administered by the theocracy of priests.

For over a century before the rise of Antiochus IV, the Judaean
province had been going through a process of "creeping Hellenization"
through the agency of the Seleucid Empire. Although the monotheistic
views of the Judaeans were not in keeping with the polytheistic notions
of the Seleucids, there was some room for "cognitive compromise." As
early as circa 300 B.C., the traveler Hecateus of Abdera notes that the
"Jews had greatly altered the ordinances of their forefathers" as a
result of Greek influence.[6] There is ample evidence to suggest that
Greek language and culture made significant inroads among the Judaean
populace, especially in the circles of the urban-aristocratic class.[7]

---

[5]For the full range of viewpoints on this matter compare Frend (1967): Chapter
2-3; Marcus' essay in Schwarz (1964), and Hadas (1965).
[6]c.f. Frend (1967:430). According to Josephus, Accataeus also mentions that
some Jews were willing to "face torture and death in the most terrible form
rather than repudiate the faith of their forefathers."
[7]c.f. Lieberman (1944) and Hengel (1974).

On the whole, this process of cultural compromise between the Hellenizers and Jews produced only minimal turbulence during the pre-Antiochan period. Admittedly, literature dating from this period, such as a book of *Zechariah,* castigates those who "contaminate" the Israelite religion with "blasphemous practices."[8] But on the whole, the period of early Hellenization of Palestine was remarkably calm. This calm gave way to a storm during the reign of Antiochus IV.

The basic goals of Antiochus' policy were to expand the borders of his empire and to weld his heterogeneous dominion into a body united by Hellenistic culture. Shortly after coming to power, Antiochus initiated a program of forced Hellenization in all provinces under his reign, including Judaea. He reportedly installed a pro-Hellenistic puppet as Jerusalem's high priest, and subsequently ransacked the treasures of the Temple. At the same time, he mounted a military campaign against the Ptolemies in Egypt. In the process, his troops overran the Judaean Province. These actions, together with the dissemination of a false rumor that Antiochus had died, led to an insurrection among the inhabitants of Jerusalem.

When Antiochus returned to Jerusalem (169 B.C.) he brutally quelled the revolt. After smashing the resistance, he reportedly initiated a comprehensive program of persecution designed to break the back of the Judaean nationalist spirit. According to the testimony of the author of Maccabees,[9] Antiochus defiled the Temple in Jerusalem, slaughtered thousands, and forbade the practice of circumcision and the celebration of religious festivals.

As is well known, Antiochus' project of persecution backfired. Instead of repressing Jewish resistance, he ignited a mass revolutionary movement which, ultimately, controlled Judaea through the Hashmonite dynasty for two centuries. Our purpose here is not to tell the story of this revolt for the thousandth time.[10] Rather, it is to examine the literary documents which were produced by Jews responding to the Antiochan repression. As we shall see, it is in these texts that the concept of martyrdom was introduced to western consciousness, and the martyr as a social type originated.

The Literary Evidence
Our examination will be based on four texts:

8c.f. Zechariah, Ch. XIV.
9See first Maccabees, Ch. 1.
10For the full story of the Hashmonean revolt against Antiochus see Brodsky (1974); Beckerman (1972); Zeitlin (1939).

1. First Maccabees[11]

This work is the most valuable and credible source of information on the mindset of Judaean nationalists during the mid-second century B.C.E. The book consists of a four-part narrative relating the history of Israel from the Hellenistic reform to the death of the last Maccabean brother, Simeon. It was written in Hebrew by a Palestinian Jew living in Jerusalem.

Most scholars believe the book was composed during the reign of John Hyrcanus I (135-104 B.C.E.). The author's obvious purpose was to defend the legitimacy of the Hashmonean dynasty by showing that the Maccabees saved the Jews from persecution, reimposed the rule of Torah, and brought to the Judaeans an era of peace and political independence.

2. The Book of Jubilees[12]

This work is an extensive elaboration of Genesis I through Exodus 12, portrayed as a secret revelation transmitted by the angels to Moses at Mount Sinai. The author's main concern is to set forth halachic concepts contained implicitly in the stories of the patriarchs.

Unlike *First Maccabees*, the author of *Jubilees* cannot definitely be placed in mid-second century Palestine. Some scholars have dated the book's final redaction as late as the sixth century A.D., while others trace its origins to Qumran during the first century A.D. There is, however, a growing consensus that the work was composed by a Palestinian Jew living between the years 168-140 B.C. Because of the controversy surrounding the date of its composition, we will not treat *Jubilees* as a reliable account of the world view of Palestinian Jews. The work will be referred to only for reinforcement of points which can be found in the more reliable sources, such as *First Maccabees*.

3. The Book of Daniel [13]

For over a century, biblical critics have argued about the date and authorship of the *Book of Daniel*. Some see the book as a conglomeration of texts written by five authors whose lives spanned five centuries. Others read *Daniel* as a unitary text compiled in its entirety in the sixth century B.C. The most prevalent and acceptable view is that of Nickelsburg (1981). He maintains that the *Book of Daniel* consists of two parts, Chapters 1-6, and 7-12.

---

[11]The discussion of the First Maccabees is based primarily on Nickelsburg (1981); Pfeifer (1949); Schurer (1973).

[12]The discussion of Jubilees relies on Nickelsburg (1981); Zeitlin (1939).

[13]The analysis of Daniel incorporates elements from Nickelsburg (1981); Ringgren (1966).

The first part relates the story of Daniel in Babylon and builds up to a climax in which Yahweh displays His unique powers and His ability to reward those Israelites who remain faithful to their religion.

The second part of the *Book of Daniel* contains a sequence of visions that Daniel allegedly saw during the reigns of Belshazzar, Darius and Cyrus. Of importance to us is that Nickelsburg claims these visions, in reality, date from the time of Antiochus' persecutions, and they reflect various events in that period. Through the use of mythic symbolism, Daniel depicts the persecution as a rebellion against heaven, and predicts the act of Divine judgement that will squash the rebellion and usher in an era of salvation. According to Nickelsburg, Chapters 7-12 were collected and attached to Chapters 1-6 by a Palestinian Jew some time during the years 167-164 B.C.

4. The Testament of Moses

Commonly known as *The Assumption of Moses,* this work was redacted some time during the first decades of the common era. However, some textual critics have convincingly argued that the bulk of the work was written by a Palestinian Jew living during the persecution of Antiochus Epiphanes. The book retells the story of the death of Moses, adding a set of secret prophecies which Moses supposedly transmitted to Joshua. In these prophecies, Moses describes the events which took place in the Antiochan persecution.

The Testament of Moses was composed either in Hebrew or Aramaic, and was later translated into Greek and Ethiopic. It is extant only in one incomplete manuscript containing a Latin translation of the Greek version. Because of the great uncertainty surrounding the authenticity and authorship of the work, it cannot be viewed as a reliable record of the sentiments of Palestinian Israelites during the mid-second century B.C. Like the *Book of Jubilees,* it must be read with extreme caution and skepticism. For this reason, we will allude to the manuscript only to strengthen a point which can be found in the more reliable sources.

The Emergence of the Protomartyr

The four diverse sources quoted above share one significant aspect: they reflect the perspective of Jews living in Palestine during the mid-second century B.C.E. From these sources we can recover the personal and collective imagination of the Israelites when they were facing religious persecution. The image of the Protomartyr emerges from the collective world view of these early Palestinian Jews.

During the Antiochan suppression there were two additional social types which emerge from the literary sources of the period. As we have explained, the social type is a category of persons who share certain collective character traits which are recognized by the community. The emergence of the protomartyr cannot be fully appreciated without a description of these other two as well: the pro-Hellenist and the zealot.

The Pro-Hellenist

Although they could be seen as flexible, open-minded individuals, willing to adapt and to "modernize," the pro-Hellenists are depicted as evil, deceptive renegades in the *First Maccabees*. In fact, all four sources offer a negative description of the social type who willingly accepts Hellenistic practices and abandons, or compromises, the Jewish worldview and way of life.

> At that time there appeared in Israel a group of renegade Jews who incited the people. 'Let us enter into a covenant with the Gentiles round about,' they said, 'because disaster upon disaster has overtaken us since we segregated ourselves from them.' The people thought this a good argument, and some of them in their enthusiasm went to the king and received authority to introduce non-Jewish laws and customs. They built a sports-stadium in the gentile style in Jerusalem. They removed the marks of circumcision and repudiated the holy covenant. They intermarried with the gentiles and abandoned themselves to evil ways.
>
> (Ch.1: 11-15). *First Maccabees.*

In the collective imagination of the Judaean nationalists, the Pro-Hellenizer embodied many negative qualities. He or she is generally depicted as a member of the aristocracy who sells out to the Hellenistic rulers. The *Assumption of Moses* has this to say about such individuals:

> They will turn aside from righteousness and approach iniquity, and they will defile with pollutions the house of worship and they will go whoring after strange gods. For they will not follow the truth of God, but some will pollute the altar with the very gifts which they offer to the Lord, who are not priests but slaves, son of slaves.
>
> (Ch.V,3-5).

Not only will the pro-Hellenic priests pollute the holy temple, they will contaminate and corrupt the entire population. Under the influence of the "pro-Hellenic scoundrels," many will shun the ways of Yahweh.

> The colony and borders of their habitation will be filled with lawless deeds and iniquities; they will forsake the Lord; they will be impious judges; they will be ready to judge for money as each may wish.
>
> (Ch.V,6). *Testament of Moses.*

The pro-Hellenizers are depicted as corrupt and greedy scoundrels who prefer their self-interest to the values of the people. Daniel describes these figures as "those who are willing to condemn the covenant" with Yahweh.[14]

The chorus of condemnation against the pro-Hellenists is amplified in Jubilees: they are described as traitors who forsake the covenant between Yahweh and his chosen people.

> For all have done evil, and every mouth speaks iniquity and all their works are an uncleanness and an abomination.
> (Ch. XXIII, 20-21).

As we can plainly see, the pro-Hellenists are described in the most disparaging terms possible.[15] In the view of Jewish nationalists during this period, they represented evil and contamination. In stark contrast to these despicable types, the same authors also speak of heroic figures. The most important of these heroes is the figure of the zealot.

The Zealot [16]

The "zealot" is a militant fanatic who would kill rather than see the Law of Moses compromised. There are certainly no lack of zealots in the world today, willing to kill others for their own convictions. The classic examples of this type are Matathias and his sons. *First Maccabees* introduces Matathias in highly dramatic fashion:

> And the king's (Antiochus') officers that were enforcing the apostasy came into the city Modin to sacrifice ... and Matathias and his sons were gathered there. And the king's officers spake to Matathias, saying ... come thou first and do the commandment of the king, as all the nations have done, and the men of Judah, and they remain in Jerusalem; and thou and thy sons shall be honored with silver and gold and many gifts. And Matathias answered and said with a loud voice, if all the nations that are in the house of the king's dominion harken unto him, to fall away each one from the worship of his fathers, yet will I and my sons and my brethren walk in the covenant of our fathers. Heaven forbid that we should forsake the law and the ordinances. We will not hearken to the king's words, to go aside from our worship, on the right hand or on the left hand.
>
> And when he had left speaking these words, there came a Jew in the sight of all to sacrifice on the altar, according to the king's commandment. And Matathias saw it and his zeal was kindled, and his reins trembled, and he shewed forth his sword and ran, and slew

---

[14]c.f. Daniel Ch. X.

[15]For our purposes, it is completely irrelevant whether or not the actual Pro-Hellenist bore any relationship to their negative stereotype. For a more balanced picture, see Hengel (1974).

[16]For a good discussion of the Zealots of Judaea, see Farmer (1936).

him upon the altar. And the king's officer, who compelled them to sacrifice, he slew at the same time and pulled down the altar. And he was zealous for the law ... and cried out in the city with a loud voice saying, Whoever is zealous for the law and maintaineth the covenant, let him come forth after me.

(Ch. I; 15-22)

After this colorful depiction, the author of *First Maccabees* relates in some detail the further deeds of Matathias and his sons. Matathias reportedly gathered around him a company of "mighty men of Israel" who were willing to offer themselves for the law. This band of zealots "smote sinners in their anger and lawless men in their wrath." They went "round about and pulled down the altars and circumcised by force the children that were uncircumcised."

Throughout the narrative in *First Maccabees*, the zealot as a social type is held up as the hero who is responsible for delivering Israel from the clutches of disaster. If we read carefully, however, we can discover an additional heroic social type lurking in the background. That figure is, of course, the protomartyr.

The Protomartyr

Having set out the characteristics of the pro-Hellenist and the zealot, we can now clearly delineate the role of the protomartyr. He or she, like the zealot, is an antithesis to the pro-Hellenist. Both the protomartyr and the zealot are willing to die rather than forsake the laws of their ancestors. But the protomartyr differs from the zealot in one crucial aspect: *he would rather be killed than kill.* Instead of striking out at the persecutors and the pro-Hellenists, the protomartyr adopts the tactic of passive resistance.

In what follows, we will attempt to set out the social setting and conceptual scheme which rendered protomartyrdom a plausible method of resistance to persecution. First, however, we will return to the texts to study their descriptions of the protomartyr.

It appears that protomartyrdom was discovered by accident. According to *First Maccabees*, a group of a thousand Israelites who sought "justice and judgement" fled to the wilderness with their families in order to avoid the Antiochan persecution. Predictably, we are told that the despicable pro-Hellenists betrayed their brethren by informing the authorities of their whereabouts.

And it was told the king's officers and the forces that were in Jerusalem, that certain men who had broken the king's commandment, were gone down into the secret places in the wilderness; and many pursued them and having overtaken them, they encamped against them, and set the battle in array against them *on the Sabbath day.* And they said unto them, 'Thus far, come forth, and

> do according to the word of the king and ye shall live.' And they said, 'We will not come forth, neither will we do the word of the king, to profane the Sabbath day.' And they hastened to give them battle. And they answered them not, neither cast they a stone at them, nor stopped up the secret places, saying 'Let us die in our innocency, heaven and earth witness over us, that ye put us to death without trial.' And they rose up against them in battle on the Sabbath, and they died, they and their wives and their children and their cattle, to the number of a thousand souls.
>
> (Ch.ll, 29-38).

In this striking account, we see many major elements of a full-fledged martyrology. The victims choose to submit passively to death, rather than forsake a normative principle, namely observance of the Sabbath. Instead of hiding, or at least resisting by force, they chose "to die in their innocency" in the hope that "heaven and earth will witness over them."

The protagonists in this drama are best seen as protomartyrs rather than martyrs. The author indicates that the slaughtered Jews were actually *zealots victimized by circumstance.* Had the battle taken place on any day other than the Sabbath, the victims might have fled or offered armed resistance. Nevertheless, the story reveals that the idea of martyrdom had begun to crystallize in the consciousness of Palestinian culture. The conclusion is reinforced by two other accounts generated in the nationalistic milieu of second-century B.C. Palestine.

First. there is the story of Taxo which can be found in the ninth chapter of *The Testament of Moses.* The chapter begins by recounting in detail the barbaric Antiochan persecution. We are informed that Antiochus' officers tortured Israelites until they agreed to blaspheme Yahweh and to worship idols. The author then goes on to describe the actions of Taxo:

> Then in that day there will be a man of the tribe of Levi whose name will be Taxo, who having seven sons will speak to them exhorting them: "Observe my sons, behold a second visitation has come upon the people, and a punishment merciless and far exceeding the first. For what nation or what region or what people of those who are impious towards the Lord, who have done many abominations have suffered as great calamities as have befallen us? Now therefore my sons, hear me: for observe and know that neither did our fathers nor their forefathers tempt God, so as to transgress his commands. And ye know that this is our strength and thus we will do. Let us fast for the space of three days and on the fourth let us go into a cave which is in the field and let us die rather than transgress the commands of the Lord of Lords, the God of our fathers. For if we do this and die, our blood will be avenged before the Lord.
>
> (Ch.IX: 1-7).

In this story, we have many elements of the classic martyrology. Taxo and his sons prefer to die passively, rather than forsake the laws of their forefathers. They offer themselves as a sacrifice, in the hope that God will avenge their blood. What is missing, of course, is the confrontation with the persecutor. If this story did in fact originate during the period of persecution, it further strengthens our claim that the concept of martyrdom began to take shape at this time. However, as noted above, *The Testament of Moses* cannot definitively be attributed to a second century Palestinian author. We are not, thus, certain that the figure of Taxo exemplifies a social type harbored in the consciousness of Judaean nationalists.

The figure of the prophet Daniel, however, definitely enjoyed a prominent position in the mindset of the Judaeans during this period, and he is an example of a protomartyr. It is not by chance that *The Book of Daniel* was redacted into its present form during the Antiochan persecution. Nor is it coincidental that Daniel is mentioned in the zealot Matathias' deathbed sermon to his sons.

With his dying breath, Matathias urges his sons to "be zealous for the law and give your love for the covenant of your fathers. And call to remembrance the deeds of our fathers which they did in their generations; and receive great glory and an everlasting name."[17] Matathias goes on to list the heroic deeds of the patriarchs and the rewards which God bestowed upon them. Last on Matathias' list is Daniel who "for his innocency was delivered from the mouth of lions."

The statement attributed to Matathias is highly significant for our analysis of protomartyrdom. It was the prophet Daniel, and his compatriots, Hananiah, Mishael and Assariah, who represent "innocent" heroes that refused to compromise the laws of their ancestors even in the face of grave personal danger.

The Plausibility Structure of Protomartyrdom

Until now, we have described the emergence of Protomartyrdom without mapping out its plausibility structure. We will now attempt to outline the social conditions and structures of consciousness which made the emergence of protomartyrdom plausible. This will enable us to understand why the martyr as a social type made sense to Palestinian Jews living during the period of Antiochan persecution.

Since the Protomartyr submits passively to death rather than compromise the Mosaic ordinances, we will now analyze why it made sense for an Israelite to die rather than compromise the Mosaic code,

---

[17]See First Maccabees, Ch. 11.

and why passive submission to death was considered a proper response to persecutions.

Willingness to Die

Considering the significance of the Mosaic code to the Israelite society, the willingness to die is not too difficult to understand. It is clearly beyond the scope of this chapter to provide a comprehensive discussion of the role of the Mosaic law. For our purposes, it may suffice to recall a few key points:

First, the Mosaic action-guide was perceived as a sacred covenant between Yahweh and his chosen people.

Second, the prescriptions of the code were intimately linked with a comprehensive interpretation of reality, including a cosmology of the structure of the universe and a cosmogony of its origins.

Third, the code was tied in with a proud national heritage and a sense of collective identity. In short, the Mosaic law was the axis upon which the Israelite's world revolved. Through the observance of its ordinances, one attained meaning, order, dignity, identity and sanctification. By forsaking these laws, the Israelite was in danger of entering a chaotic, meaningless and polluted realm.

It is important to note that at the time of the Antiochan suppression, there were strong apocalyptic currents circulating among the Judaean populace. Many Jews believed that the persecutions were merely a final drama before eschaton. At that time the "remnant of the faithful" would be delivered, while the apostates and the heathens would be smitten. In addition, the Antiochan persecution prompted the Israelite writers to speak of collective resurrection for those who die in defense of the law. This notion, coupled with a belief in the eschaton, would surely have enhanced the plausibility of life sacrifice for the covenant. As G.F. Moore has written:

> The emergence of the idea (of resurrection) in the persecution of the religion by Antiochus Epiphanes and the insurrection of the faithful Jews in its defence, was at an opportune moment ...[18]

Another view which undoubtedly contributed to the plausibility of self-sacrifice was the notion of a battle between opposing deities. This concept, taken over from Iranian religion, may have led some Israelites to see their persecutors as messengers of an evil force opposed to Yahweh. As Frend notes,

> In the last chapter of Daniel, Antiochus himself is seen not merely as a hostile ruler but as a contrary power to God. He was cast

---

[18]G.F. Moore (1950 Vol. II, p. 314); c.f. Hergel, (1974: 196-202); Mac Greggor (1936: 129-142).

for a supernatural, demonic role, the first antichrist. In the writer's view, the struggle between Judaism and Hellenism becomes part of a cosmic drama, at the end of which the victims would rise from the dust of the earth and shine as stars in the heavens and their opponents, the Hellenizers and apostates would awaken to shame and everlasting contempt. Judgement would award each according to his merits.[19]

Given all these ideas circulating in the Judaean orbit, Antiochus clearly erred when he forced Israelites to choose between forsaking their law or dying for it. By forsaking the law, the Israelite stood to lose both his present world and his hopes for the future. By sacrificing himself for the law, he could die a meaningful and holy death, thus assuring himself a happy future in the age to come.

Our analysis of the plausibility structure which lay the grounds for sacrificing one's life would not be complete without taking cognizance of the social and class interests underlying these elements of consciousness. The evidence regarding these interests has been a matter of fierce scholarly debate for the past half century. There are two points, however, that can be made with relative certainty.

First and foremost, we must recall that the religious suppression posed a mortal threat to the social order of Judaean society because the entire social fabric rested on the Mosaic law code and the Temple cult which it generated. Among those dedicated to the continuity of the social order, Antiochus' threat was a real one. It created a climate of fervent support for those willing to kill and to die in the resistance to religious suppression. The situation was a classic illustration of the Durkheimian principle that the social order rests ultimately on the willingness of persons to make sacrifices. Had all the Israelites agreed to Antiochus' decrees, had the Zealots and protomartyrs not been activated, the Judaean society would not have been maintained, and the Moses law code would have disappeared.

Secondly, there is some indication that those willing to die for the Mosaic code, namely the zealots and the protomartyrs, belonged to a rural, agricultural class. This class strove to uproot the more well-to-do urban pro-Hellenists. There were, thus, class-related material interests which fused with the religious convictions.

In our view, it would be an historical injustice to "reduce" the fierce conviction which activated the zealots and the protomartyrs to either the protection of class interests or a defence of the social order. It is important to point out the "fit" between these factors, but the relative priority among these determinants cannot be adequately verified with the sparse and problematic data available to us. Until the dust of

---

[19]Frend (1967: p. 38).

scholarly debate on the period settles, or until new data is uncovered, we believe that what we have presented about the congruence between the social order and the plausibility structures of martyrdom is all that can responsibly be claimed.

Passive Sacrifice

The protomartyr's tactic of passive resistance is more difficult to explain than the mindset and the social circumstances which rendered sacrifice for the law a plausible course of action. From our study of the classical texts, we have concluded that it was the elements embodied in the prophetic-apocalyptic literature, and in the priestly code which contributed to the path of passive resistance. It is our thesis that the protomartyr was viewed as an innocent sacrificial offering designed to atone for the sins of the people.

The idea of vicarious atonement through sacrifice had been firmly established in the consciousness of the Israelite populace through the rituals of animal sacrifice in the priestly code. It was accepted that the death of an innocent animal could vicariously atone for the sins of the Israelite people.

> There is ample evidence to show that an atoning function was attributed to or associated with almost every kind of sacrifice; indeed atonement was seen to be the purpose par excellence of sacrifice, and this atonement was seen to be affected primarily through the blood rites.[20]

Vicarious atonement is based on a fairly simple metaphysical assumption. It is presumed that sin produces divine anger which inevitably leads to punishment. Through the ritual of sacrifice, God's anger is directed away from the sinner toward an innocent, whose vicarious suffering absorbs the sinner's punishment.

Although human sacrifice was never officially incorporated, the Old Testament books such as Deuteronomy, are full of examples in which innocent persons suffer or die in order to placate God's anger against sinners. This notion is most explicit in the apocalyptic prophetic works. The four stage theodicy systematically employed in these works include: sin, suffering, the turning point, and salvation. It is the turning point which, in most cases, involves the suffering of innocent persons.

The idea of vicarious suffering reaches its closest approximation to protomartyrdom in the Deutero-Isaiah. This source explicitly speaks of an innocent witness who atones for the people's sins through his

---

[20]Dely, 1978, p. 87 c.f. Notes.

suffering and death. The most significant passage, of course, is the oft quoted Isaiah 53:10-12:

> We had all strayed like sheep, each of us had gone his own way; but the Lord laid upon him the guilt of us all. He was afflicted, he submitted to be struck down and he did not open his mouth; he was led like a sheep to the slaughter ... After all his pains he shall be bathed in light, after his disgrace he shall be vindicated; so shall he, my servant, vindicate many, himself bearing the penalty of their guilt.

We do not know whether this particular text formed part of the plausibility structure of second century protomartyrdom. However, there can be little doubt that the apocalyptic literature, the Deuteronomic theodicy and the cultic sacrifices played a major part in rendering protomartyrdom a plausible response to persecution. By the second century B.C., the Israelite consciousness contained the notion that innocent death can atone for sin and expedite divine deliverance.

The plausibility structure of protomartyrdom also included a set of social interests which we will now examine. It is clear that the protomartyrs, particularly those depicted in *First Maccabees*, served the vital interests of the Judaean nationalists who led the revolt against the Seleucids and the pro-Hellenists. They sought to win over the loyalties of all Judaean inhabitants who were ambivalent, and thus, the opponents of the revolt were portrayed as thoroughly evil. By slaughtering passive Judaeans together with their wives and children, the Seleucids and pro-Hellenists handed the Maccabeans a stunning public relations victory. As Klapp (1974:86) points out,

> Martyrdom is a dramatic strategy that cannot lose; the resister being passive, is extremely hard to see as a villain, while the opponent, whether he wins or not, can hardly avoid being cast as an aggressor by an open minded audience.

From Protomartyrdom to Martyrdom

From the world of the Judaean nationalists, we now shift to the Hellenistic Jews living on the periphery of Palestine several generations after the Maccabean insurrection. Unlike their compatriots in Judaea, the Jews living in Antioch and Alexandria lived as a tiny minority in a world dominated by Hellenism. Within this context, the Jews carved out a "cognitive compromise" with their polytheistic neighbors. "Hellenistic Judaism" was the compromise produced by a creative synthesis between Greek and Israelite culture.

As a member of a relatively powerless minority, it was natural for the Hellenistic Jew to look back towards the glorious days of the Maccabean insurrection. We thus find several works written by Hellenistic Jews recounting the events of the Judaean revolt. It is in these works that the concept of martyrdom first comes to fruition. In order to trace how this idea took shape, we must recall that the Hellenistic Jew was firmly rooted in Greek culture. The heroic ancestors of the Jews in Alexandria were seen through glasses tinted with Hellenic imagery. It was these images which provided the vital elements needed to transform the protomartyr into a martyr.

In the mindset of Hellenistic Jews, three key social types which contributed to the emergence of martyrdom can be isolated. The first is the figure of the warrior-athlete, a heroic individualist who faces pain, and even death in order to overcome his opponent. The second is the philosopher (exemplified most perfectly by Socrates), who stoically stands by his rational principles, regardless of the personal expense. Finally, there is the tragic figure (e.g. Antigone) who chooses to die, rather than forsake a normative principle. These three images, together with the Greek notions of an afterworld and a disembodied soul, were the crucial elements of consciousness needed to consolidate the figure of the martyr. It is thus hardly a coincidence that the first martyrologies were created by Hellenistic Jews.

In order fully to appreciate this point, let us briefly examine the books of *Second* and *Fourth Maccabees*.

1. Second Maccabees [21]

The second book of Maccabees, according to the testimony of its anonymous author, is part of a larger work composed by Jason of Cyrene. The book provides a detailed history of the Maccabean revolt. It is prefaced by two letters in which the Jews of Jerusalem urge their brothers in Alexandria to observe the festival of Hannukah. The book's author was probably an Alexandrian Jew living during the reign of Alexander Janeus (103-76 B.C.). Writing in Greek for an audience of Hellenistic Jews, the author incorporates all the classical elements of the rhetorical, pathetic narrative. Through vivid drama and macabre descriptions,[22] the composer of *Second Maccabees* seeks to elicit empathy for the struggling Judaean Israelites.

Much as in *First Maccabees*, the Zealot is portrayed as a national hero, but here his position is less significant than the new national hero; the martyr. Four discrete martyrologies can be isolated in the text. The first two are similar to the accounts of protomartyrs which we explored earlier. We are told of two women who were brutally killed

---

[21]This analysis relies mainly on Nickelsburg (1981), Hadas (1953), Pfeifer (1949) and Schurer (1973).

[22]A significant indicator of the impact of Second and Fourth Maccabees on classical martyrdom is the etymology of the word macabre, which derives from the word maccabee.

because they defied the Antiochan prohibition against circumcising newborn babies. These women were led around Jerusalem with their babies hanging from their breasts, and then were "cast down headlong from the walls" of the city. The author of *Second Maccabees* also retells the story of the zealots who refused to fight on the Sabbath. In this version however, the zealots were "all burnt together" in a cave.

These protomartyrological accounts set the stage for the entrance of Eleazer and Hannah, the first true martyrs. The Story of Eleazer runs as follows:

> Eleazer, one of the leading scribes, a man of advanced age was being forced to open his mouth and eat pork. But he, welcoming a glorious death in preference to a life of pollution, went up of his own accord to the torture wheel, setting an example of how those should come forward who are steadfast enough to refuse food that it is wrong to taste even for the natural love of life. Those in charge of that unlawful sacrificial meal, because of their longstanding acquaintance with the man, took him aside and privately urged him to bring meat provided by himself, which he could properly make use of, and pretend that he was eating the meat of the sacrifice, as the King has ordered, so that by doing this he might escape the death penalty, and on account of his lifelong friendship with them be kindly treated.
>
> But he, making a high resolve, worthy of his years and the dignity of his age and the hoary hair which he reached with such distinction, and his admirable life even from his childhood, and still more of the holy and divine legislation, declared himself in accord with these, telling them to send him down to Hades at once. 'For,' said he, 'it does not become our time of life to pretend and so lead many young people to suppose that Eleazer, when ninety years old, has gone over to heathenism, and to be led astray through me, because of my pretense for the sake of this short and insignificant life, while I defile and disgrace my old age. For even if the present I escape the punishment of men, yet whether I live or die I shall not escape the hands of the Almighty. Therefore by manfully giving up my life now, I will prove myself worthy of my great age, and leave to the young a noble example of how to die willingly and nobly for the sacred and holy laws.'
>
> With these words, he went straight to the torture wheel, while those who so shortly before had felt kindly toward him became hostile to him, because the words he had uttered were in their opinion mere madness. As he was about to die under their strokes, he said with a groan, 'The Lord, in his holy knowledge, knows that, though I might have escaped death, I endure dreadful pains in my body from being flogged; but in my heart I am glad to suffer this, because I fear him.'
>   (Ch.VI:18-31)

Immediately following this dramatic tale, the author of *Second Maccabees* provides yet another martyrology. The protagonists are Hannah and her seven sons. Hannah is forced to look on as each of her sons chooses to endure pain and death, rather than eat forbidden food.

One by one, the sons are subjected to hideous tortures. Each of them goes to his death willingly and passively. With their final breath, the children express confidence that they will be resurrected and that their persecutors will be punished. Some of them mentioned that they are dying for the sins of their people. They express hope that their innocent death will arouse God's mercy and put an end to the persecution. After the youngest son is put to death, Hannah herself follows her sons to eternal glory and resurrection.

In these dramatic stories, the primitive notion of protomartyrdom gives way to a fully developed martyrological theology. The martyr is held up as a role model for all Jews suffering from persecution. He or she is seen as a virtuoso of religious conviction who will be rewarded with eternal glory in the afterworld. The martyr's death is perceived as an innocent sacrifice which will atone for the sins of the Israelite people and thereby expedite divine deliverance.

As the image of the martyr comes into focus, the Zealot fades into the background. In *First Maccabees*, Matathias and his sons are responsible for Israel's salvation. In *Second Maccabees*, by contrast, the death of the martyrs marks the turning point which arouses God to end his people's persecution.

This shift in emphasis can be explained from a sociology of knowledge point of view. As a minority living in a Hellenistic world, the Jews of Alexandria could not accept the Zealot as a role model. The zealot's adherence to the law was, of course, a crucial value for the Jewish minority seeking to preserve its self-identity. But all other aspects of the zealot's world view reflected dangerous and inappropriate values, since the zealot stood for armed resistance to heathenism. In Alexandria of the first century B.C., such an attitude could only lead to group suicide.[23]

For the Hellenistic Jews, the martyr was a more appropriate figure to embody normative Jewish values. The martyr had all the heroic stubbornness of the zealot without his dangerous militancy. Instead of taking up the sword, the martyr put his or her faith in heaven. This was surely a more appropriate tactic for the circumstances of the Hellenistic Jew.

In order to further illustrate this point, let us briefly examine *Fourth Maccabees*.

---

[23]This same tension between zealotry and martyrdom is true in many different historical periods. For a perceptive treatment of it in the Middle Ages, c.f. Cohen (1965) *Messianic Postures of Ashknazim and Sephardim.*

2. Fourth Maccabees [24]

The *Fourth Maccabees* was composed by a learned Hellenistic Jew living in Antioch during the reign of Caligula (37-41 B.C.). It is written as a rhetorical discourse designed to illustrate "that religious reason is sovereign over the emotions." The bulk of the work is devoted to the deeds of Eleazer, Hannah and the Seven brethren, while the deeds of the Hashmonean Zealots are given only a cursory treatment. In style and content, the book marks a synthesis between Platonic dialogue and Euripidean tragedy.

Eleazer is portrayed as a true "philosopher," patterned after the figure of Socrates, and Hannah is described in terms reminiscent of the Greek Iphigenia, whom we will describe in Chapter Five. The actions of the martyrs are depicted as a battle on behalf of virtue, or an athletic contest to be endured. The moral of the book is that the Jews are a nation of martyr-heroes with deep religious convictions. Judaism, the combination of philosophy and martyrdom is seen as the most genuine form of Jewish heroism.

The stories of *Second* and *Fourth Maccabees* represent the culmination of a long chapter in the history of ideas. In these martyrological stories a roughly sketched figure located on the periphery of Judaean consciousness is transformed into a vivid image embodying the central values of Hellenistic Judaism. Through a complex process of development, the desperate Judaean protomartyr evolved into a stoic-philosopher hero.

Although the martyr-related figures we have examined make up a wide range of divergent types, they shared one basic characteristic. All were willing to submit to torture and certain death, rather than compromise on practices and convictions which were deemed normative by Mosaic Law. This single-minded stubbornness surrounds the martyr with a halo of "archaic dignity," but one is inclined to understand the view of their persecutors who saw them as completely mad. Objectively, the actions attributed to Eleazer were highly irrational. But when one enters the subjective world of a martyr's culture, it can seem plausible to commit suicide over a piece of pork.

It is unthinkable to conclude our chapter on the origins of martyrdom without a reference to Christianity. It was the martyrdom of Jesus and the legacy of the early Church which enabled the idea of martyrdom to enter the mainstream of western consciousness. Although Christian doctrines of martyrdom are grounded in a theology largely

---

[24]The analysis of Fourth Maccabees relies on Nickelsburg (1981), Hadas (1953) and Emmet (1918).

foreign to pre-Christian Judaism, there are several points of contact between the martyrological traditions of the early Church and the Judaism of late antiquity. Abundant material exists which indicates that the martyrs of the early Church were influenced by Jewish figures such as Daniel, Eleazer and Hannah.

As Frend writes:[25]

> What inspired the Christian to go to his death was the tradition of Hebrew righteous suffering ... without the Maccabees and without Daniel, a Christian theology of martyrdom would scarcely be thinkable. The Christian, living, suffering and dying as a witness to the Living Christ, believed that he was fulfilling the hopes which had inspired Old Israel since Maccabean times.

There is no doubt that, in the imagination of many early Christians, Jesus represented the pinnacle in a long tradition of Hebrew martyrdom.[26] We do not know enough about the historical Jesus, however, to know how much his view of passive and innocent suffering was influenced by the Judaean idea of protomartyrdom. We can only say with certainty that, at the time of Jesus' crucifixion, the notion of vicarious suffering and passive response to persecution were firmly embedded in Judaean consciousness.

Discussion & Summary

In this chapter we have attempted to trace the origins of the martyr as a social type. During a particular historical period and under a particular set of circumstances the martyr became an accepted expression of non-negotiable community convictions which had been cruelly challenged. In our analysis, we have endeavored to demonstrate the dynamic and multi-faceted aspects of the martyr's origins.

Implicit in our analysis is the assumption that the martyr's development cannot be understood without tracing the parallel development of the pro-Hellenist, the zealot, the protomartyr, the warrior athlete, the philosopher and the tragic hero. As a social type, particularly in the early stages, we have shown that the martyr was not a fixed entity, but rather a product of prior types that had evolved, and a response to specific social circumstances.

Beyond the period of origins, this same dynamic quality continues to accompany the development of the martyr subsequently. Post Constantinian Christianity brought with it a redefinition of the martyr's role. The sexual abstinency of the monk replaced bodily sacrifice as an equivalent manifestation of martyrdom . This continuing

---

[25]Frend (1967) pp. 56-71.
[26]c.f. Malone, *The Monk and the Martyr* (1978).

process of evolution reinforces our thesis that, as the community values and convictions change, the martyrological expression of these convictions change as well. Both the martyr and the community are in a continuing and dynamic process of transformation. We believe that it is crucial to take a historic approach to the study of social types. Only by analyzing them in their historically specific context can one see how they are a changing expression of, and forceful influence on, their social environments. We also believe that the study of the martyr as a social type can contribute to our understanding of the role of conviction in the evolution of culture. This in turn will help shed light on the dilemma of modern man in an age of loosening community bonds, and a fear of commitment.

Part Two

MARTYRDOM AND THE
PLAUSIBILITY OF CULTURE

3

The Martyrological Confrontation and the Impact of Uncompromising Conviction

The publicly observed death of a martyr serves a social purpose. It is an ultimate statement of commitment to the group and what that group represents. In this chapter, we will discuss the impact of the martyr on the plausibility of culture; on the early stages of group formation; and on the social construction of commitment.

The Plausibility of Culture

There is a fragility to human meanings, particularly with regard to the central questions of existence: What is the purpose of life?; What is the most suitable way to live?; Who are our friends and who are our enemies?; How do we explain misfortune and tragedy?

Providing answers to these primary questions cannot be the task of solitary individuals only. Cultures and religions have evolved out of a deep need for response, and each provides its own characteristic answers. The edifices constructed to provide meaning in life and answers to these questions are forever fragile and transparent. The firmness of their structural supports are based on mere human agreement. They only appear to be rooted in the nature of things. They exist, in reality, by human fiat. No matter how impressive and solid the edifice of meaning, its transparence reveals the arbitrary human beliefs that undergird it. In the end, it is the inescapable structural transparency that generates doubt about culture and commitment.

How can one silence these doubts?

One of the ways is to link the answers to something of undisputed importance, human life. It is not by accident that the origins of culture are associated with human sacrifice and killing. There are fundamentally two alternatives that human beings have in response to the implausibility of life meanings. They can either sacrifice their own lives (or the life of someone dear to them) to demonstrate the importance of these meanings, or they can kill those who attempt to challenge them.

The second alternative demonstrates the importance of meanings by destroying all those who challenge their plausibility. It attempts to destroy the challenge by eliminating the challenger. The possibility of doubt, however, is perpetuated because killing others in order to achieve greater security of belief is an intrinsically bloody business with no natural end. There are always others around to doubt and to challenge.

With the first alternative, however, doubt is ended. Once a believer has been sacrificed for a belief there is no longer a way to challenge or to doubt that belief. Dying for one's beliefs, strangely enough, ensures the continuity of one's convictions, and more humanely than through killing.

The martyr serves as a key to understanding the problem of making culture plausible within the human condition. For is not the reality of death the central issue in the project of making cultural achievements plausible? What is the worth of human achievement if it perishes? The most existentially fateful contest is between the hopes and aspirations of human beings on the one hand, and their mortality on the other. Between entities which are lasting, and beings who are perishable.

Through his or her death, the martyr makes believable those abstract principles that lie at the root of human connectedness, such as kinship, religious belief, national or ethnic solidarity or the more universal principle of "humanity." We are forced to take note of the martyr's conviction because it appeared true, valid and convincing enough to warrant self sacrifice.

However, everything would appear to have a price, and here the significance of the martyrological confrontation becomes apparent, in our view. It is only under extreme duress and coercion that most people would be willing to pay with their lives for recognized and validated principles, and the martyrological confrontation presents just such duress and coercion. The martyr willingly pays with his or her life for convictions that are publicly challenged, controversial and lack the stamp of societal legitimacy. In situations where oppressors are suffocating in the staleness of their traditional forms, the martyr represents a breath of fresh air. His or hers is a daring, impressive assertion of character, particularly and paradoxically in the eyes of the persecutor. As one of the characters says in Fry's "This Lady is not for Burning" (1950), "Come let us burn her before she converts us."

The impulse for creating culture and the building of symbolic realms of meaning is related to man's fear of mortality.[1] Through the martyr's capacity to conquer mortality with a cultural commitment, he or she holds a special fascination for us all. The martyr is a contestant like the rest of us. Only he is out there in the arena braving the direct confrontation while the rest of us are quietly struggling in less exposed ways. The symbolic power of the martyr consists in his fighting the universal fight, around a culture in the early stages of creation or in the process of revitalization.

The martyr's claim to fame is based on his or her willingness to be exposed to the universal struggle between the basic drive for biological survival and man's deep need for a life of conviction. In the public arenas, he is willing to be seen suffering the agony of the contest between these two formidable forces.

This public struggle forms the basis of the martyr's posthumous victory. Unlike animals whose capacity for altruistic self sacrifice is genetically linked, human beings can choose to sacrifice themselves for groups that are in the process of formation. This choice is at the heart of the social purpose of martyrdom.

The martyr, consequently, is relevant to issues of social change, to cultural struggles, to man's attempt to live by self proclaimed values and principles, and to group formation.

Confrontation, Martyrological Conviction, and Group Formation

Martyrdom is a social event intimately connected with the formation of groups and the strengthening of group identity. The most effective legitimation for a newly formed group is an example of dramatic conviction staged in a confrontational public setting. Within the context of group life, conviction itself is both validating and contagious. The martyr is the virtuoso of conviction and, as such, is the most effective catalyst for the creation of a convictional community. By validating the group's convictions and demonstrating their hold in the most trying circumstances, the martyr seems to proclaim that these convictions are strong enough to conquer the fear of death.[2]

---

[1]Exploring the relationship between the creation of culture and the fear of mortality are the following: Ernest Becker: *Angel in Armour, The Denial of Death; The Structure of Evil,* Edith Wyschograd, *The Phenomenon of Death, Faces of Mortality.*

[2]McClendon and Smith in *Understanding Religious Conviction* explore the importance of overcoming the fear of death, and its role in what they call "interconvictional encounters." p. 174.

It is precisely these impressive qualities that have been used by group founders to support, buttress and legitimate the purposes for which their groups have been formed. After all, how many ways are there to justify and validate the convictions which lie at the root of a new group's formation?

An attempt to validate the group on the basis of "naturalness" is the tactic of well established, not newly formed groups. In the early stages, some other basis of validation is needed. Appeal to the self interest of the members is problematical because in their initial stages groups tend to take more from their members than they give. Alternatively, the group can be validated by what it gives to non-members (i.e. 'our group has a right to live because of what it does for others'), but new groups tend to be more predatory and self serving than altruistic.

There is, thus, a universal affinity to martyrdom during the early stages of group formation. Martyrs are to be found in the formative stages of religious sects (Noss, 1957); political parties; newly created revolutionary cadres (Laqueur, 1977); schismatic movements (Lifton, 1971), and even terrorist gangs (Laqueur, 1971). Let us now seek to analyze this affinity.

The Psychological Component[3]

According to Girard's psychoanalytic theory of group formation, a martyr's dramatic strengthening of the group bond is due to the primal link between birth and sacrifice. This link is based on an echo of a primitive association in the human mentality and sensibility (Girard, 1972). According to the psychologistic mythic view, new existence seems to demand as its price some diminuation of vitality in the creative generative force that brought it into being.

From this perspective, it is essential that the creative force apologetically demonstrate some sacrifice of itself and its achievements, lest some potentially more destructive and jealous power be aroused (i.e. the "evil eye"). In order to protect the vulnerable new birth from punishment for the creator's past wrongs and offenses, some sacrifice and expiation are required. There is a need for gestures of placation, submission and single minded devotion in order to offset the pride and intoxication associated with creating something new.

Thus, just at the moment of creative fulfillment, there seems to be a mythic, unconscious requirement that part of the creation – the best part – be sacrificed in order to insure the remainder. This requirement lies buried in man's pre-history and in his early religious development,

---

[3]Our thinking about martyrdom has been influenced by Riddle (1931).

and, as such, is exceedingly difficult to substantiate with verifiable evidence.

The evidence brought forward to support this claim is that in many primitive religions one finds sacrificial rites associated with renewed creation. During the known history of mankind, individual self-sacrifice has been associated with the formative stages of social groups.

The Sociological Component

From a sociological point of view, there are at least five ways in which the martyr contributes to a group's formation and survival:

1. A Dramatic Focus of Attention

On the whole, human beings tend to go about their daily business relatively oblivious to grand historical purposes. This has been true throughout most historical periods and in most human societies. The relatively rare moments of collective enthusiasm come about generally in times of crisis such as war, revolution, or acute economic or social stress. Martyrs also serve as a dramatic focus of attention.

As Fraser (1978) has pointed out, there is an inertia in human societies which strongly resists change. Most people need to be convinced that it is worthwhile or necessary to devote either interest or energy to the formation of a new group. Getting past that tendency to resist change requires first of all an attention to the new.

The martyrological confrontation, like the screaming headline in a popular newspaper reporting a murder or a rape, evokes attention. Martyrdom is far from a routine matter in most societies. People do not generally sacrifice their bodies for a principle. Nor do they tend to show courage in the face of torture and death. Curiosity is aroused as to what could have been the commitment which led to such sacrifice. Martyrdom evokes an interest that leads beyond the here and now.

The curiosity and interest aroused in bystanders and spectators as to the meaning or motive for the sacrifice serves an important purpose for the group. Recruitment of new members requires that the group become a focus of attention and interest and the martyrological confrontation can serve just such an attraction.[4]

2. The Crystallization of Group Purposes

Martyrs help to crystallize group purposes which previously may have been inchoate or poorly focused. Martyrdom within the public confrontation is frequently accompanied by memorable statements of

---

[4]The capacity of martyrdom to engage observers and rivet their attention to the act of sacrifice is explored empirically by Melvin J. Lerner.

conviction; famous last words. These convictional statements, preserved and valued because of the dramatic circumstances in which they were uttered, are typically short, clear utterances that epitomize the cause or principle for which the martyr sacrificed him or herself.

In addition, the martyr provides greater credibility to the group purposes. His or her sacrifice is a living proof that the group has a purpose worthy enough to elicit extreme acts of loyalty.

3. The Feasibility of Defiance

Martyrs dramatize the feasibility of defying an oppressor when facing coercion. The martyr demonstrates that defiance is thinkable and doable through the challenge of superordinate, oppressive power. He or she breaks through the tacit acceptance of established authority and its right to determine public policy by decree. A martyr can thus become the contagious example of courage which can be imitated by individuals in any oppressed group inclined to rebel in the name of a principle.

Not only do martyrs demonstrate the feasibility of defiance, they also bestow upon this defiance a dignity and an appeal through the arousal of guilt in their contemporaries. Those who do not follow in the footsteps of the martyr are both elevated and diminished. They are elevated by the thought that they too can choose to be martyrs, and diminished by the fact that they may choose not to do so. The very possibility of moral heroism makes moral cowardice more palpable, and its acknowledgement inescapable.

Through their example, the defiance of authority becomes a kind of moral imperative, a value in and of itself. "Defy authority like me," the martyr seems to say. Not because in so doing the authorities will be immediately overthrown, although that surely will happen in the long run. Defy authority because defiance is tantamount to self respect.

This appeal to feelings of guilt and to the arousal of a moral imperative is not merely instrumental and pragmatic. It also has an absolute quality to it. No temporary improvements that the superordinate powers might institute could possibly alter the fundamental inner compulsion by martyrs to show defiance towards coercive power in order to gain individual and group self respect.

4. The Demoralization of the Persecutor

In the long run, martyrs tend to demoralize their persecutors if they persist in their martyrological sacrifice. There are a number of reasons for this phenomenon. Persecutors, like all the powerful, prefer that their subordinates internalize their demands without the necessity for confrontation and for coercive enforcement from above. Such coercion involves the expenditure of energy and resources.

Power tends to atrophy or to drain away, and the need for constant enforcement is a draining process. If the authorities are to successfully maintain their power, they need steadfastness and discipline. The martyr's steadfastness in his or her cause, his loyalty to it, and his unwillingness to compromise in the face of confrontation are all qualities which the powerful covet. These are the very qualities they seek to cultivate in their loyal subjects.

The persecuting ruler would like to see his own purposes elevated and embraced rather than the uncompromising opposition of the martyr who is loyal to a different cause and a different group. There have been moments in history when persecutors have demonstrated their fascination and ambivalence towards martyrs by pointing to their loyalty as an example of the loyalty they themselves demanded from their subjects. They have even been known to do this at the moment when they were putting the martyr to an agonizing test.

This ambivalence displayed by persecutors has not escaped the attention of martyrologists. In the long run, the demoralization of persecutors is a direct result of such ambivalence. For it is not only the existence of people who defy him which thwarts the persecutor. If he had only the task of enforcing his will and asserting his power, then he would succeed as long as he had access to the means of coercion. These means are not sufficient because the undermining process initiated by the martyr is ultimately more dangerous to the persecutor.

While there is no doubt that the sheer exercise of coercive power arouses feelings of intoxication (since it dramatically illustrates just how powerful one is); in the long run, however, it must lead to exhaustion. This exhaustion gradually leads to doubts about the legitimacy of power in the minds of the authorities, their supporters, and ultimately in the minds of their less rebellious coerced subjects.

5. The Transformation of the Deviant Label

Martyrs are labeled as deviants by the oppressing power. However, through the acknowledgement of such deviance and through its glorification, the stigma of deviance is changed into a badge of honor. The confrontation with deviancy transforms it into the prideful proclamation of a prized identity. By publicly acknowledging the deviance and showing pride in it, the entire group can identify with the proclamation and the martyr's act is no longer aberrant. The act of martyrdom is thereby not the deviant act of isolated individuals, but the quintessential expression of the group's values.

6. The Measure of Group Devotion

After their sacrifice, martyrs continue to serve as a measure of group devotion and commitment. This is the price exacted from future adherents to the group. It is a standard of loyalty to the group's convictions. The martyr's sacrifice implies that, according to the group's norms, this is the ideal demonstration of conviction. A loyal member is defined by implication as a person willing to sacrifice him or herself just as the martyr did. In other words, at the initial stages of group formation, martyrdom sets standards for praiseworthy acts that become standards for continued group membership.

The message is communicated to future group members that membership in this group is a serious, fateful enterprise which may demand the ultimate sacrifice. New members are thus prepared from the beginning for the possibility of paying a high price for their membership. The very act of joining such a group involves a momentous decision. Acts of conformity to the group's norms are then almost a foregone conclusion, and group attitudes and behavior tend to be aligned with the high costs which are potentially involved.

Put succinctly, if a group has a martyr to a martyrological confrontation during the initial stages of its formation, it is highly probable that the group will be dedicated, disciplined and focused on purposes that are pursued relentlessly. Riddle (1938) calls this group capacity Social Control, and it will be discussed in Chapter Four, in our analysis of the martyr's motive.

The Social Construction of Conviction

By being willing to suffer and to die for his or her convictions, the martyr produces two simultaneous, important effects. The established beliefs in society that have been accepted in the past are challenged, and another new set of beliefs are made more plausible and compelling. With the same act of self sacrifice, the early Christian martyrs both challenged the legitimacy of Emperor worship, and affirmed that Jesus was God incarnate.

The Validation and Falsification of Beliefs

The martyrological contest can be viewed as a contest about what is true, or, more exactly, what should be true. It is about the question: who defines what people should regard as truth, which "folk knowledge" should prevail. Since folk knowledge is the belief system that is taken for granted by the members of the community, successful martyrdom makes a different set of convictions plausible and transforms them into an acknowledged reality of life.

Folk knowledge differs from scientific knowledge, with its built-in rules of validation. The scientist's beliefs are based on empirical research, which can be tested and refuted in clear and accepted ways. Folk knowledge (the accepted folk truth), on the other hand, tries to avoid testing through the use of clever stratagems and is mostly validated by being taken for granted. Since falsification can be particularly dangerous, it is not always clear how folk truths can be disproved.

The martyr's act within the martyrological context can put folk knowledge to the test. The assured status of commonly held beliefs is undermined through challenge from a competing set of beliefs.

An important point to note here is that falsification is inherently more powerful than validation. This is true both in the case of scientific knowledge and of folk knowledge. Falsification has more finality and conclusiveness than validation. A Syrian friend who did graduate work in the United States once went home on vacation. During the course of an altercation, he said "no" to his patriarchal, traditional father for the first time in his life. His father left the room in dismayed anger and the relationship between them has never been the same. One act of negation was enough to signal the father that his authority had been challenged in ways that were irreparable. This one act of negation falsified the routinely accepted supreme authority of the father. Both father and son understood this.

Hegel points to the same factor in the relationship between Master and Slave. Within the first act of negation lie the seeds of rebellion and revolution. Our carefully constructed worlds of social fact require constant validation. We need to agree on the basic belief system in order to function in society. Falsification of these basic beliefs is devastating. This is as true in the world of scientific knowledge as in the world of social norms and folk knowledge.

Popper has pointed to the peculiar vulnerability of even the scientific fact. The proposition "all swans are white" gets scant confirmation from the discovery of one more white swan, or even a hundred, or a thousand. However, let one black swan be discovered, and the statement is falsified once and for all. No matter how many white swans are then discovered, they can not dispel the lingering doubt that perhaps tomorrow a black one will appear.

The martyr is a self styled black swan. By challenging the accepted, prevailing belief system, the martyr introduces doubt and starts a process of falsification. As we have seen, falsification has a more direct, powerfully convincing effect than acts of validation. This is as true of folk knowledge as of scientific knowledge.

Established, accepted beliefs are readily reinforced through the use of ritualized validation ceremonies. This, however, is not true of non-conventional beliefs. The extraordinary or non-conformist belief requires a more powerful validation in order to be considered plausible. In order to get a hearing, it must sound an octave higher than the regular chorus of societal validations.

The martyr's act in the confrontational context is efficacious because it both validates and falsifies on an octave higher note. A contest is forced between the prevailing truth and that of the martyr's conviction. Through an act which is contrary to human nature, through suffering agony for a principle, the martyr demonstrates a willingness to put his or her own cause to the test of validation. At the same time, the gauntlet is thrown down on conventional beliefs. "Kill me, for I will not affirm your truth." Killing the martyr is a means of validating accepted truths, of "one more white swan." The martyr's challenge, however, is a presentation of a black swan. Unlike scientific knowledge, where one person can be right and a million wrong, in the matter of folk knowledge, the quantity of believers makes a difference. If enough people believe that the martyr has made a case for the black swan, the falsification of previous beliefs sticks. And since the martyr, potentially speaks symbolically for eternity, it is a dangerous voice to have around.

The validation of a cause through an act of martyrdom is final and conclusive in a way that the validation of scientific beliefs or knowledge cannot be. After the death of the martyr there is no danger of recanting. Once the crown of martyrdom is bestowed, the process is "sealed" forever. The only danger to the validation is the danger of reinterpretation and historical debunking. To prevent this, successful martyrs usually have cadres of martyrologists and hagiographers in each generation who are prepared to defend their integrity and motives. Christian martyrs have had their protectors from Eusebius, Robus, and Crespin Foxe, to the Bollandist Priests. Jewish martyrs are fixed forever and celebrated in liturgy and classical Talmudic sources. In all tradition, everywhere, there are watchful authorities on guard for defamations and desacralizations of their acknowledged martyrs.

The Sacralization of the Cause

In addition to validation, the martyr's cause inspires reverence because he or she was willing to die for it. If we analyze the phenomenon of reverence, we find in it elements of both awe and devotion. These are the feelings we bestow on the sacred, and both these elements are worthy of our attention.

Awe is the most appropriate response to the presence of mystery. As Wheelwright has indicated; "Mystery is no puzzling riddle with a solution to be published in next Sunday's supplement, it is that which intrinsically and majestically transcends the possibility of finite comprehension." There are extraordinary events of nature, or terrible human tragedies which overwhelm us and inspire awe. However, unlike martyrdom, these events do not also inspire devotion, the second indispensible aspect of reverence. Devotion is the result of our own questioning exclamations for which we expect no answer.

Reverence is the religious attitude that is framed in the "irony of its own finitude."[5] Martyrs and their convictions are intrinsically religious phenomena because they evoke awe and devotion in the group. They are humanly finite, but are tied to transcendent and eternal aspirations and pretensions. When the martyr's cause succeeds, it then symbolizes the group.[6] From the perspective of the social scientist, this transformation from controversial nonconformity to sacred conviction is no small matter. What we have pointed out is, it can be achieved through the self-sacrifice of an individual for his or her own conviction in the face of a public confrontation.

From Opinion to Social Conscience

On less mysterious and more mundane levels opinion is transformed into conviction through the agency of martyrdom. It is the conviction and the perseverance of the martyr which becomes the conscience of the community. The remarkable social journey from opinion to belief and then to conviction is one of increased subjective certainty. It is a willingness to stake more and more of oneself on the fact that one believes oneself to be in the right.

By witnessing the sacrifice of a fellow human being for a conviction, others learn to stake their existence on an opinion. The martyr's awesome display of conviction is a powerful lesson that opinions can and should be fateful. This is a frightening lesson which no doubt scares many prudent types away. But there are many people who are attracted to the possibility of having greater certainty about things.

The martyr evokes a conflict in spectators between the need for safety and the need for certainty. We seek group values, but it is only through the seriousness with which individual beliefs and convictions are held that they become transformed into group values. Yehudah HaLevi claimed in the Kuzari that Judaism is correct because there were so many martyrs, and Origin claimed that Christianity was true because people were prepared to die for it. It is the willingness to sacrifice for them which distinguishes deeply held convictions from "mere opinions."

There is an inevitability about the need for martyrdom in order to bolster conviction and generate certainty. As Samuel Johnson has written: "I have got no further than this: Every man has a right to utter what he thinks truth, and every other man has a right to knock him

---

[5]Wheelwright, The Burning Fountain, p. 295.
[6]c.f. Emile Durkheim, The Elementary Forms of Religious Life.

down for it. Martyrdom is the test." How then, does one get the courage to hold convictions which will cause one to be knocked down hard? Through the emulation of revered martyrs and, as we shall now discuss, through the support of fellow believers. Those that are resolute in their beliefs help one another.

The Ascendancy of the Resolute in the Face of Confrontation

One of the paradoxes of martyrdom is that the group is strengthened when individual members die as martyrs. It is, of course, a commonplace that people tend to cling together in times of trouble, and persecution is trouble. However, when people are willing to endure life threatening dangers for the sake of their convictions, there is a certain winnowing out of those with lesser conviction. In groups where martyrdom is prevalent, it is precisely this winnowing process which strengthens the remaining members. The disaffection of those with weaker beliefs makes the group stronger. Not in numbers, but in the degree of conviction of the remaining members. Those lacking in conviction are frightened away while the believers become more uncompromising. This process of winnowing and strengthening could be called the ascendancy of the resolute.

When groups experience the ascendancy of the resolute, it is a powerful process which encourages extremism and lack of compromise. The effect is that martyred groups become more entrenched and recalcitrant, which further arouses opposition, confrontation and continuing martyrdom. It seems that such martyrdom could continue indefinitely, but it does not. Changes take place which bring an end to the martyrdom:

1. The persecuting group uses up its resources and capacity to punish and repress.

2. The martyred group is destroyed or severely crippled through the death of its leaders.

3. The persecuting group capitulates and adopts the values of the martyred group.

4. Martyrdom is transvalued and defined as something other than the seeking of death to test resolve.

5. Other strategies of opposition are adopted instead of martyrdom.

There are historical examples for each of these resolutions; the Romans grew tired of persecuting the Christians. They had used up enormous resources for this purpose and in the end they adopted the religion of the persecuted; the groups of martyrs in the concentration camps were utterly destroyed and their example lost because all their witnesses were also put to death; martyrdom was transvalued and redefined by the medieval church to include the sacrifice of sexual pleasure for the sake of religious principle. One did not have to die in order to become a martyr. Maintaining habits of sexual abstinence won the crown of martyrdom as well.

Without the ascendancy of the resolute in the face of confrontation, and without suffering persecution and martyrdom, groups tend to include many members with weak commitment. It is the persecuted and martyred groups, as we have indicated, who have a higher percentage of dedicated members. This constitutes a clear danger for the persecutor. Creating a martyrological confrontation can only lead to greater conviction in the surviving members of a persecuted group. For those in power, this is certainly a situation to avoid. Nothing has as strong an impact on the potency of groups that are losing their core values as some persecution and the possibility of offering martyrs for the cause.

The ascendancy of the resolute brings forth dedicated new leaders in groups facing persecution. In more peaceful times, leaders ascend to positions of power not necessarily because of their convictions, but frequently because of their organizational skills. However, in a situation of conflict between groups, leaders are called upon to demonstrate conviction. Those leaders who cannot show the depth of their conviction through personal example, are delegitimated. The same holds true for rank and file group members. In a contest of conviction, it is the strength of conviction that counts. Persistence in conviction works its power on both members and spectators in the long run.

How, then, do the resolute maintain their resolution? The answer seems to bring us back to the function of the martyr as an example for the rest of the adherents. The guilt and feelings of obligation aroused by the sacrifice communicate to the group members that they are expected to do their bit as well. It is a process which resembles price raising mechanisms in the market. For the privilege of continued participation in the group, the price is raised. Adherents incur debts to the group because of the martyr's sacrifice, and the group is empowered to call in those debts. In other words, through the martyr's sacrifice, the group is empowered with a moral right to make additional demands of commitment and of energy from the members. The group has an interest in keeping the memory alive, in case of the need for future sacrifices from members. The memory of the martyr's sacrifice helps to keep members in line.

The martyr's depth of commitment creates a situation in which his or her own life comes to an end. It is however an ending which purports to be a new beginning, one which gives greater validity to convictions. In the process, when martyrdom is successful it challenges and disconfirms established beliefs. These disconfirmed beliefs lose their effectiveness in holding people in their thrall. The martyr validates principles for the living, by dying. As Kermode has reminded us, "... tracts of time unpunctuated by meaning derived from the end, are not to be borne."[7] The Martyr's end, in the situation of confrontation, addresses this human anxiety in very profound ways which effect the plausibility of culture, the formation of groups, and the social construction of conviction in society.

---

[7]F. Kermode, *The Sense of Ending*, p. 162.

4

The Martyr's Motive and the Formulation of Conviction

We have discussed the impact of martyrological conviction in the face of confrontation, on the formation of perceived truths in a culture and on the early formation of groups. The question we now pose is related to the martyr, him or herself. What is the source of the martyr's staying power under conditions of supreme stress? The issue is basically one of identification with a cause and the implications of that identification on the martyr. In this chapter we will present a sociological analysis of the martyr's motive.

Our concern with motive, as we shall shortly see, is not necessarily according to expectations. Unlike the psychologists and psychoanalysts, our focus is not on the intrapsychic processes of the martyr psyche. Our concern, instead, is what the martyr and others *say* is the motive.[1] In our analysis, we wish to remain within the sociological discipline, although the temptation to stray from this framework is great. It seems that everyone has something to say about martyrs and martyr motivation.

Towards a Sociological Analysis of the Martyr's Motive[2]

Motive seems such a supremely psychological category. What could a sociologist say about motive which could not be better said by a psychologist? The fact is that psychologists have had a great deal to say about the martyr's motive, particularly with regard to pathology.

---

[1]c.f. Peters, *The Concept of Motivation* (1958); Mills, C.W. "Situated Actions and Vocabularies of Motive," (1940); Turner, J. "Towards a Sociological Theory of Motivation" (1982).
[2]Lyman and Scott, "On Accounts."

Psychologists have tended to reduce all of the martyr's behavior to motives rooted in psychological disturbances.[3]

The psychological position which perceives motives as spring-like mechanisms has been associated with deterministic orientations. These orientations view human action as constrained or determined by internal impulse (or in the case of behaviorists, by external circumstance). The actor is impelled to act by forces that impinge on intrapsychic process. What the actor says about his or her motivation is suspect and of little consequence. If these declared motivations were regarded as true, there would be little for psychologists and deterministic sociologists to add. The inclination is to find "deeper," mysterious motives, of which the actor is unaware. Finding these hidden motives is a kind of professional imperative for the psychologist.

The sociological discipline suggests a perspective from which the martyr's motives can be perceived. Unlike the psychological perspective, in which motives are seen as mechanisms springing from the black box of self, which mysteriously cause subsequent action; sociological perspective views motives as the way in which the self and others perceive and organize the action of social actors in order to make that action more understandable. This perspective involves a careful look at what martyrs say and do.[4]

In the sociological perspective, the concern is not to find the "true motive," whatever that may be, but to describe the process to which motives are ascribed and imputed to actors. The question of truth or falsity about the "real motive" is here suspended. Concentration is focused on how perceived motives are constituted, and how social actors are understood by others and themselves. There is not necessarily a contradiction between the two approaches, but there is a significant difference in the focus of concern. While the psychological approach dictates an exploration of the martyr's psyche, the sociological approach views the motive as part of social interaction, i.e. the seeing, talking and theorizing[5] in which the martyr and the society around him or her engage.

According to the sociological approach, the search for motive is not conducted among the hidden springs and impulses which cause action. It

---

[3]e.g. Menninger, *Man Against Himself* (1938); Lubin, A.J., *The Life of Vincent Van Gogh – Stranger on the Earth* (1975).

[4]Lyman and Scott, "On Accounts"; Blum and McHugh, "The Social Ascription of Motives."

[5]c.f. Blum: Theorizing (1973), especially Chapter 7, "Commonality and Communality," pp. 185-218.

is rather an analysis of how actors in the midst of action seek explanations, assign meanings and differentiate themes; how these actors decide what is happening to themselves and others; whether these explanations are persuasive in social interaction; and how effective they are in advancing interests and making people feel they understand what is going on. It is this second sociological perspective which will be the framework of our discussion of the martyrological motive.

Motive and World View

It is virtually impossible to act in the world without a view of what one is about, a view of what motivates oneself and the other. Human beings do not act like unprogrammed Golems in a motiveless world. We construct theories about what we and others are about, and we motivate ourselves and others to understand what we do and are done to. This task of motivating the world is an act of social construction.

We do not go about this work alone and in a vacuum. We are helped by our stock of knowledge about cultures, societies and our immediate contemporaries. We know why we and others do things, because we are products of a culture. Motives are the property of culture, languages, myths, and worldviews. They have various degrees of credibility according to the social situation, and depending on who is announcing them. There is a grammar of acceptable usage according to who is being addressed. A politician convicted of fraud would offer one set of motives to his constituents, another to his psychiatrist and perhaps another set to himself.

The social search for motive in ordinary interactions generally involves a strong predisposition towards finding something that has been predetermined. Discovering motives is done by people who know how to find them, and in this we are all experts. It is an expertise we acquire in order to act in the world, to be competent. In a sense we are all like the dishonest policeman who looks for the best place to "plant" the drugs he has in his pocket, in order to collect the proof he needs against his suspect, and to make his own incriminating testimony more believable in a court of law.[6]

In most social interactions, we already know who we are dealing with and why they do what they do, before we start the interaction. What we search for is confirmation. Lacking such confirmation does not necessarily deter us. We find ways to confirm what we know by ascribing a priori knowledge, imputing it, or simply fabricating it. As

---

[6]The example is from Blum and McHugh (1974).

we shall see in our analysis of the manipulation of conviction (Chapter Five), in the case of Horst Wessel, Goebbels "knew" Wessel was a martyr, despite all evidence to the contrary. He managed for many years to convince the German people that what he "knew" was true.

The grammar of motives is a set of rules governing the social acceptability of certain kinds of "plants" in specific situations for certain kinds of people. There are motives which are acceptable in some contexts but not in others. There are also certain ways to speak according to the circumstances, and if one does not follow the accepted rules, one may not be understood. While we know that Wessel was a fraud and Goebbels the incarnation of evil, the millions of Germans who sang the Horst Wessel song while shedding sincere tears apparently did not. This reality is enough to give both the value that people place in the sincerity of motive, and martyrdom a bad name.

Sociologists regard with some skepticism the assumption of the psychologistic view that a particular motive can be universal in all persons. Nothing in the sociological perspective corresponds to the sex motive which is impugned to be universally present in all humans. Motives are viewed by the sociologist as the concrete product of particular social groups. There is no way to anticipate which aspect of an action will be singled out and given the recognition of a socially acceptable motive.

Napoleon is reported to have said that if you want to motivate people to fight and die, don't give them principles, give them baubles. Napoleon's army conquered most of Europe, and he may have been right for his time and place, but baubles would not necessarily be sufficient in a different era. During the Vietnamese war a large portion of the population in the United States did not seem to find baubles a sufficient motivating factor for the fighting.

If there are motives that seem to be widespread or even universal, the sociologist demands an empirical demonstration. In order to prove that martyrdom is a universal phenomenon, one must look at all societies and groups over all of recorded and even pre-recorded history. Our aims, however, are more modest. We wish only to suggest that martyrdom is a phenomenon that can be found in the societies and groups that we know something about. We do, however, have our suspicions that the phenomenon is indeed universal. We have thus revealed ourselves to be the apriorists we have accused all others of being. We take some comfort in the fact that, according to some contemporary philosophers, such a priori assumptions are apparently necessary if one wants to understand the world.[7]

---

[7]Hesse, M. "Theory and Value in the Social Sciences" (1978).

We now turn again to the question as to whether sociologists can tell us anything that we did not know about the martyr's motive. Is there anything fundamentally social about the self-sacrifice of individuals for a cause, or is it simply the psychological aberration of individuals who are susceptible to epidemics of masochistic frenzy? In order to address these questions, we will consider four situations where there are areas of interplay between the subjective dispositions of the martyr (i.e. the psychological motives) and the social circumstances.

1. The Socially Validated Martyr's Motive

These are situations where the martyr's motive is self proclaimed and also socially validated (e.g. The classical martyrdom of the Jews during the Hellenistic period and the martyrdom of the early Christians).

2. The Socially Validated, Non-Self Proclaimed Motive:

In these situations, the martyr him or herself either repudiates the acclaimed motive, or is indifferent to it, but the act of martyrdom is socially validated (e.g. this would appear to be the case with Martin Luther King Jr.).

3. The Self-Proclaimed, Non-Socially Validated Motive

These are the individuals who claim to have martyrological motives, but their motives are not socially validated. There are many mental hospitals which seem to have candidates that fill this definition. An important qualification here is that at some future time validation may indeed occur (as in the case of Joan of Arc).

4. The Non-Self-Proclaimed, Non-Socially Validated Motive

This category includes the rest of mankind. It must, of course, be taken into consideration that at some time in the future social validation may be given to an individual who did not proclaim a martyr's motive and his or her death was not socially validated when it occurred. The most blatant example of the reversibility of this category is Goebbels' resurrection of Horst Wessel.

The Proclamation of Martyrdom

The proclamation of a martyr's motive is accomplished in a variety of ways. In classical martyrology, an explicit statement of motive is publicly made to the effect that: "I am willing to forfeit my life rather than submit to this decree which violates my principles." The statement is made in a situation where transgression of the decree is known to be punishable by death. However, the motive can also be proclaimed symbolically. This was the case with Becket who indicated his willingness to imitate Jesus and die as a martyr by appearing at a celebration of the first Christian martyr, St. Stephen, carrying a cross.

The proclamation can also be made by a group which does not include the martyr. Bestowing the moral dignity of martyrdom through the impulse of a group, can take place whether the individual actually deserves such recognition or not. Bullock writes that towards the end of World War II, when the German Generals were plotting to kill Hitler, Rommel opposed the plan. He claimed that if Hitler was assassinated before he was brought to trial and convicted, the German people who supported him would make him into a martyr.

When martyrdom is validated by social circumstances, but not self proclaimed by those who were killed, it is generally suspect. "True" martyrdom requires some evidence, even fabricated, of the martyr's willingness to die. For example, despite the proclamations made by Israel's Memorial authority (Yad VaShem) as to the martyrdom of those Jews who died in the Nazi concentration camps, doubts as to the validity of this status are constantly raised.

Since life does not flow according to the logic of analytic typologies and other heuristic devices, there is usually an interaction between the self-proclamation of the martyr, who persists in his or her principled nonconformity, and the social circumstances. People do not always proclaim what they believe. There is a tendency to proclaim only what one believes will be validated by significant others, or what will be harmful to enemies. In these cases the proclamation of motive is based on the anticipated social effects.

The martyr's proclamation is not only the result of an impersonal encounter between an implacably opposed will and an irreconcilable cause.[8] An equally important consideration is the individual's rational evaluation of the social impact of taking a dangerously controversial stand. This is certainly the case with Socrates as described in the Crito and the Phaedo. Socrates was willing to die because, according to his own calculations, if he violated his own principles he would have a bad effect on those around him and severely compromise the principles for which he himself stood.

Eleazer, the Jewish Hellenistic martyr, refuses to eat the "pretend" pork to save his life because of the bad effect on his students. The same is true of martyrs throughout history. A cold logic can be seen in the evaluation by some of the Christian martyrs as to the effects of their actions. To see the phenomenon of martyrdom mainly through the framework of implacable wills which are in conflict, and irreconcilable

---

[8]This appears to be the view of Victor Turner, *Drama, Fields and Metaphors* (1974).

causes, places the martyr's motive beyond rational calculation. The martyr's decision to sacrifice his or her life is often based on a rationally grounded belief that the principle he or she represents will live because of the sacrifice.

The early Christian martyrs came to the conclusion that Tertillian gave expansion to: "The blood of the martyrs is the seed of the church." The more Christians willing to die, the greater the chances that the Church will live. (This was in the days before humanity developed the capacity for mass extermination and genocide.) The martyr, thus, is not always an irrational believer. He or she can be a calculating social reformer willing to risk his or her own life in order to have an impact on humanity. There are times when it is rational to die for one's values, depending, of course, on what those values are.

The Social Validation of Martyrdom

Although the origins of the martyr's motive can be understood either psychologically or through the language of social grammar, the validation of that motive is hardly a psychological question. Such validation is a social process requiring the cooperation of a range of people over considerable periods of time. It is symbolized by official recognition.

The forms of social recognition include: the bestowal of a title, the incorporation of some ritual, canonization in an approved list, or inclusion in a body of literature especially constructed to perpetuate the memories of the martyrs. It can also be through the construction of a monument or a plaque, or in the form of a social movement or a religion that arises as a response to the martyr's sacrifice. These forms of validation all involve social processes. The Jesuit priest Herbe Thurston has aptly described this process:

> There is a popular impression, an impression shared even by some Catholics that the process followed in the beatification and canonization of saints is analogous to that by which the Sovereign creates a Knight of the Garter or raises a commoner to the peerage. The analogy, if it exists at all, is a very imperfect one, for it suggests that the initiative in this conferring of spiritual dignities come from the Pope and not from the people. The assumption is that a Vicar of Christ, having honors to bestow in the Church triumphant as well as in the Church militant, causes search to be made among the available records in order to discover the most worthy recipient of his favors. According to this mistaken view the Sovereign Pontiff fixes his choice upon this one or that who has died in the repute of sanctity and then after a certain measure of inquiry declares the servant of God to be 'Blessed'. Supposing that this is well received and that further miracles are reported, canonization follows in due time, and the candidate thus approved is proclaimed worthy of universal veneration.

An investigation of past history ... will show that the idea thus outlined is almost the reverse of what actually happens and of what in fact has always happened since the beginning. It is not the Pope who is anxious to 'make saints'; but the people who have to be restrained from making them too easily. The impulse comes not from above but from below. The faithful of some particular locality, impressed by the virtue and the sufferings and the miracles of one who has lived in their midst are convinced that he must be dear to God and are eager while invoking his intercession to pay him such honor as their devotion suggests.

In the earliest centuries it was the martyr who alone evoked this popular enthusiasm but soon it was realized that a martyrdom which was lifelong and self imposed might be even more worthy of admiration than that which was terminated by a single blow of the executioner's sword ... to this day the majority of the feasts which stand in the calendar of the Roman missal commemorate saints who had no other canonization than that which is involved in this general approval.[9]

Thurston's description of the way in which martyrs come into being shows a process mediated strongly by social definitions and negotiations. Many different groups have a hand in the creation of the Catholic martyr. The validation process involves the influence of popular culture which includes: the dramatization of a life, the diffusion of the legend, the generation of a myth, the bureaucratic processing, certification and authorization, and a suitable ritualization. Creating a Catholic martyr involves plain people, narrationists, myth makers, bureaucrats, clergy and masters of liturgy and ceremonies. Even when the primary pressure for the creation of martyrs is from below, it must flow to the top of the hierarchy before it can be validated.

The Limits of Social Control

The social validation of the martyr's motive depends on the support of a group. It is unlikely that most martyrs would be able to sustain their motivation without a supportive group. What then are the limits to this support? Can the group get an individual to do anything? Does human nature not impose some limits to suffering, sacrifice and commitment? There appear to be no such limits.

It has been claimed that the sociological perspective tends to overlook the unchangeable self-preservative givens of human nature and credits the group with omnipotent powers of socialization. For sociologists, the case of the martyr's motive is a particularly interesting example of the impact of such group powers. After all, let it

---

[9]Thurston & Altwater, *Butler's Lives of the Saints* (1952), pp. 667-668.

not be forgotten that the end result of such group socialization is an individual's willing self- sacrifice. There is ample documentation and a flood of data to support the claim that successful socialization enables the martyr to be constant in affirming the cause.

The influence of the group over the martyr was noticed over fifty years ago by Riddle, but the theoretical significance of his observations was not fully realized.

> It is not to be thought that martyrs in any significant numbers could have undergone their fate if they had been abandoned in it by their fellow Christians. They were able to meet their crises only because they were members of societies which kept effective the influence of their social bonds. That such influence was operative before and during the time of confession, and even after the confession had been secured, while the confessor lay in prison or actually, as he fondly supposed, after his faithfulness unto death, accounts for the maintenance of the martyr's courage. In other words he was enabled to emerge through the painful course of punishment because he was one of a number. He was such a person as he proved to be because of group influences, of which for this purpose his Christian fellowship was the most effective. It was because of his integration as one of a group, that he was thus controllable. The essential factor in control was the influence, variously applied of the group.[10]

Riddle's comments strongly emphasize the role of the support group for the continuing motivation of the martyr. With such power attributed to support groups, sociologists who analyze the role of the social group in human motivation question what, if any, are the limits to these group powers. How far can they go in attaining human conformity to their pressures?

Despite the accumulating sociological evidence that group pressures have no limits in their impact on human motivation, sociologists seem to have lost their nerve in presenting their case.[11] During the past few decades sociologists have been far less aggressive in their claim that social influences are the most determinative elements in human behavior. Objections to this oversocialized view of human behavior come from three main sources:

1. The Psychoanalytic Orientation Toward Social Control

The psychoanalytic claim is that there is an unsocializable residue of unconscious forces, needs and inclinations in the individual which defies "total socialization" no matter how strong the pressure of the

---

[10]Riddle, D.W., *The Martyrs, A Study in Social Control* (1931), p. 101.
[11]Wrong, H. "The Over Socialized Conception of Man in Modern Sociology" (1961).

group towards conformity. These residual forces have tended to be overlooked by sociologists and therefore, according to this view, sociological descriptions of socialization processes appear to lack depth.

2. The Social Change Orientation Toward Social Control

In advanced industrial societies, change is ubiquitous and persistent. No body of cultural norms can be sufficiently situationally specific to allow for complete socialization due to the ubiquity of change. In these special circumstances, socialization becomes a preparation for ambiguity and change. Although this arrangement does not prejudge the possibility of "complete" socialization, it offers a moral argument as to the impact of the continually changing circumstances of modernity.[12] We will encounter these continually changing circumstances once again in our final chapter when we attempt to deal with the problems of commitment in the therapeutic age.

3. The Improvisational Orientation Towards Social Control

According to this approach, everyday interactions are characterized by their qualities of open-endeness, lack of structure, and unpredictability. People cannot be socialized to react in totally predictable ways, and social reality is an improvised construction created anew in each human interaction. Successful socialization in society is achieved when the individual is taught how to align behavior to the social scenes of which he is a part.[13]

This alignment, while patterned, is not wholly predictable. There is no way to learn it once and for all in all situations. (Stokes and Hewitt, 1976, 838-849). The improvisational orientation claims that all one can hope for in a socialized group is for people to become more or less competent. There will, of course, be those who are not competent at all.

A variation of this point of view, which is based on empirical investigation, states simply that societal norms do not provide absolute guidance for action in particular situations. Unlike the other views which locate the limits of socialization within the individual, or in the nature of society, this view places the limits of socialization in the

---

[12]c.f. Riesman et al, *The Lonely Crowd* (1954).
[13]Hewitt, J.P., Stokes, R. "Disclaimers" (1975) *ASR*; Blumstein, P. et al, "The Honoring of Accounts" (1974), *ASR*; Blum and McHugh, "The Social Ascription of Motive" (1974), *ASR*; Stokes and Hewitt, "Aligning Actions" (1976), *ASR*.

values and norms themselves. This intrinsic lack of specificity in the values and norms cannot be corrected or reversed.[14]

According to these three prevalent views, as we have indicated, there are limits to the power of social control and group socialization which are due to the intrinsic qualities of the unconscious, to the vagaries of the changing world, or the lack of norm specificity. In light of these objections sociologists have become more humble than they were in the days of Parsons and the heady, limitless socialization theories. Sociologists no longer assume that social forces are determinative of *all* a person's actions. What is more, they now assert that such forces can never be totally determinative.

It is, however, no less an affirmation of the importance of human freedom to acknowledge the awesome potential of groups to control their members without limit. The question of such limits should at least be asked, and the evidence of whether, indeed, such limits exist, should be evaluated. Freedom may actually become more precious in light of society's limitless potential for control over human behavior.

And how are we to explain martyrdom as a social phenomenon? It does seem to confirm that social control has no limits when a person is willing to die rather than disappoint the group. Martyrdom is a test of the limits of pain, suffering, patience, courage, loneliness, endurance and sacrifice that individuals are willing, indeed choose, to endure, with the aid of the group.

If Riddle is correct, all this is impossible without the group. Consequently, if instinctual drives towards self preservation can be overcome by social influences at specific times and places, then how can it be claimed that unconscious forces ultimately determine behavior? It seems that the alleged limits of group socialization are not very limiting with regard to martyrdom.

We believe that martyrdom raises a serious challenge to those who claim there are intrinsic limitations to the socialization of individuals. When reading the martyrological literature, one does not find those unconscious areas of the human psyche that are totally resistant to group socialization. Unless one suspects that all martyrological accounts are fraudulent, it appears that individuals can be motivated by groups to forego the most fundamental impulses of life. Mothers seemingly accept the voluntary death of children; beautiful people willingly give up their youthful potency; old people sacrifice their few remaining days for the cause; children denounce parents; every type of suffering is seemingly gladly endured.

---

[14]Cancian, F., *What Are Norms? − A Study of Beliefs in a Maya Community* (1975).

Where are the limits to what people will forego for a group value which is deeply believed in? From reading martyrologies it seems clear that the human being is essentially a social being with a limitless capacity for socialization.

The two main arguments against the sociological view of unlimited socialization and social control, though widespread, are challengeable. The first argument as to the residual aspect of the human personality which resists socialization, is not verified in the case of martyrdom. Of what possible social consequence are the fantasies and unconscious strivings of people if they are going to their death as martyrs? Their inner lives may not be totally controllable by social forces, but their actions lead them to self sacrifice. There are even indications in recent literature that emotional reactions may be more socially programmed than we have tended to think.[15]

The second objection to the concept of unlimited socialization is based on a hidden preference for freedom and autonomy. Although there is considerable truth to the claim that social reality is unplannable and social interaction largely unknowable in advance, there remain situations where interaction can be anticipated. This is particularly true in formal and ritualistic interactions.

People living in modern societies generally anticipate situations where prior socialization does not specify the proper conduct. This is quite understandable in terms of the pace of social and technological change. However, this is not the way things have always been or must be in the future. The degree to which informal interaction takes place in a society is itself a socially defined reality. Both formal and informal interactions are given a defined place in society, and are thus a further affirmation of unlimited socialization.

To underestimate the awesome power of socialization is to underestimate the amount of harm and possible good that it can do. If we choose to be suspicious of socialization attempts and do not value them we are entitled to say so, but let us give socialization its due. It's power is virtually limitless.

The Martyr's Motive and Membership Morality

Martyrs generally adopt their motives through recognized and socially certified participation and identification with an oppressed group. Our question is not how masochistic impulses find outlets in martyr-like behavior, but how groups like the Judaeans during the period of the Maccabean revolt, and the early Christians got people to

---

[15]Kemper, T.D. "Social Constructionist and Positivist Approaches to the Sociology of Emotions" (1981) *AJS*, vol. 87, number 2.

announce their martyr's motive and persevere in it until death. The question we are asking is how groups and social movements socialize their members to both profess the martyr motive and then sustain this motive until the act of self-sacrifice.

The early Christians are the best example of the interrelatedness between membership and motive. Among these early Christians a willingness to publicly avow the martyr's motive became an essential qualifying requirement for membership into the group. This avowal remained a means of maintaining solidarity with the group. Symbolically rehearsing the martyr's motive was a prime means of keeping the group vital, and it occupied a place of centrality in group gatherings. All other aims became secondary. It alone became the touchstone by which commitment and conformity to group goals could be measured.

In the process of becoming the quintessential prerequisite of group membership and loyalty, the moral ideal became indistinguishable from group membership itself. This is a process which occurs in any group with a well articulated central value, and has been described by many.[16] It is a process whereby an abstract moral ideal is transformed into a qualifying trait for membership in the group.

Once the fusion of the moral ideal with membership takes place, the group has achieved a great advantage in terms of its ability to control its member's behavior. All appeals for conformity, or sanctions against non-conformity can then be made on the basis of an appeal to group loyalty and prior membership commitment. Sin is transformed thereby into disloyalty and treason. Social morality becomes social ontology. The "ought" of morality becomes the "is" of social existence. As Piaget, basing himself on Durkheim, has indicated: "Morality presupposes the existence of rules which transcend the individual, and these rules could only develop through contact with other people."[17]

A word of caution is in order regarding the correspondence between membership and morality. Situations change, membership is fluid in groups and, not unexpectedly, morality changes. The fixity of moral purpose is sometimes compromised instead of enhanced by the association with membership. Redefinitions of the original purposes, indeed radical transformations, are inevitable as membership in the group changes. While the original moral purpose has great authority because of the importance of its founders, its hold is not absolute. Wise is the leader who inaugurates change in the name of original values.

---

[16]c.f. Durkheim, *Suicide* (1915).
[17]Piaget, *The Moral Judgement of the Child* (1962).

Under the cloak of their authority, as long as contemporary members agree, virtually anything goes.

The Sustaining of Martyr Motivation

We now turn to the question of how persecuted groups have succeeded in sustaining martyr motivation. The most complete historical record we possess of how a group organized itself to handle martyrdom, is that of the early Christians. Since their records constitute a veritable instruction manual in what we call a strong program of socialization, it would be useful to review their methods.

While we cannot claim that these methods would be equally useful for any group seeking to encourage martyrdom among its members, it is reasonable to assume that some of the major features would be relevant. The analysis of these methods has conveniently been set forth by D.W. Riddle (1931).

Riddle essentially relates the issue of motivating martyrs, to the larger question of how social groups regulate themselves and maintain *self determination*. This process of self determination includes:

a. maintaining the importance of ones own group values rather than those of other groups;

b. maintaining and continually adapting ones own set of norms to circumstances which are then legitimized by the group;

c. repudiating the coercive acts of other groups and neutralizing them;

d. maintaining order within ones group while change is taking place;

e. handling the conflict that results from a lack of articulation between ones own group and the other groups with which it interacts.[18]

All these elements and others like them have most recently been brought to our attention by the late Morris Janowitz.[19] He has claimed that these constitute a cluster of problems which he, in the tradition of Riddle and the Chicago School, conceptualizes as problems of social control. How do these problems relate to motivating the behavior of the martyr?

First of all, the historical occasions when martyrs arise are usually at a point of conflict between two groups. These conflicts generally take place in one of the following three circumstances: When a nascent group,

---

[18]Riddle, D.W., *The Martyrs, A Study in Social Control* (1931).

[19]M. Janowitz "Sociological Theory and Social Control" (1975), *AJS*.

which has been banned, attempts to form (the formative situation); when a social movement is attempting to reestablish or revitalize itself after being presumed moribund or after being banned (the reformative situation); or when existing groups are attempting to achieve hegemony over the same population (the Zero-sum competitive situation). In each of these situations, and during the ensuing conflict, the maintenance of group discipline is required for success. Only through such discipline can the group maintain itself in the presence of a threat to its integrity.

Martyrdom is a response to the challenged integrity of the group. The act of the martyr proclaims that life is not worth living if the values of the group are denied. This is the strongest possible affirmation of the group's capacity to represent reality for the adherent. The martyr's act demands that we confront the question of the group's dominion over its members.

In the terminology of the Early Church the contest with the authorities was over the Christian's confession of allegiance to the Church. Through such confession he or she would bear witness and prove devotion to the Christian discipline in the face of cruel intimidations and torture.

It is generally assumed that the major motivating force for the early Church martyrs was the promise of eternal reward in the hereafter. While this was certainly a factor in the encouragement of martyrdom, it is our contention that it was only one of a number of factors at work. Although there are many cultures that believe in a hereafter, very few succeeded in motivating as many martyrs as the early Christians. The problem with the hereafter caveat is that it purports to answer the very question it begs. Why should a promise of a blissful life in the hereafter be so efficacious? The explanation disregards the strong hold that human beings have on life. It assumes that the promise of life in the hereafter is powerful enough to motivate self sacrifice. This appears to us a gross oversimplification.

When, in fact, one analyzes the methods used to control the martyr's behavior, one finds an array of factors that are unrelated to the promise of life in the hereafter.

Some of these factors are as follows:

1. Careful visualization

The martyr did not enter a situation that was unknown to him. As far as possible, all stages in the process leading to martyrdom were anticipated and rehearsed. These stages included the arrest, the imprisonment, the physical deprivations, the examination of threatening statements by the magistrate, the attempts at persuasion, the offer of acquittal should the martyr recant, the test of loyalty in the form of performing approved rites of worship, the torture, and the various forms of death.[20] One might think such careful anticipation of suffering would intimidate rather than arouse the summoning of courage. This may have indeed been the case for many who were attracted but did not join the Church. For the motivated, this was not the case.

2. Descriptions of Successful Martyrdoms

It was particularly effective and important to provide information to all Christians about the success of martyred Christians in the confrontational arena. It served as an example of imitatable behavior. The successful martyrs were role models for all believing Christians, and martyrologies were widely circulated as part of the liturgy of the early Church.

This process had a double function. It both imparted information as to what was expected in the confrontation with enemies of the Church and it glorified that behavior which was necessary in each aspect of the martyrological confrontation. This visualization and rehearsal was particularly important in moments of confrontation. We have of late discovered that pre-rehearsal is the foundation of all self help therapies. Peers who have to face the same problem, such as alcohol, drugs, terminal illness, etc. counsel and prepare others to deal with the trials of withdrawal, abstinence or certain death.

Virtually all of the early Christians were either martyrs or were preparing themselves for martyrdom. Without exemplars, careful visualization only raises anxiety, while only exemplars without rehearsal does not provide the necessary information to cope successfully. Both parts of the message are needed. When the two factors are present the group has managed to create for its members a socialization program that more fully prepares them for a life 'in extremis.'

3. Emphasis on Observability

Every effort was made to insure that the group would witness the events leading up to the martyrdom. It was not uncommon for fellow Christians to visit the accused in their cells and to bring food and clothing to make the imprisonment more bearable. There were even celebrations to dramatize the forthcoming test of faith. These supportive efforts both brought comfort and help in a most trying situation, and had a latent message for the martyr-designate, "what

---

[20]c.f. Riddle, op. cit. p. 21.

you do and say will be observed and recorded." In a word, it will be significant and passed down in ritual form and celebration.

All martyrs were on stage. Some suffered remorse and recanted but those who could take the pressure were assured of eternity, at least in the memories of the survivors. What is distinctive about the martyrdom was not only the promise of reward in the hereafter, but the certainty of being memorialized in this world. The martyr saw before dying that he or she had earned a place in the memories of the survivors and in the liturgy of the Church. Hope, as it were, was based on certainty. There was hope in the promise of the world to come, but the martyr saw with his own eyes that he was already memorialized in this world.

Being observed can energize. To be seeable is to make the act more doable. Collective enthusiasm can bring one to do things thought impossible. We do not really know why performance in public, particularly in difficult and demanding physical and emotional situations, should raise the overall level of performance. This is certainly true of athletes. Somehow, in the public eye the individual can let loose with all the extra reserves of energy and capacity to endure suffering.

In addition to this rather mystical infusion of collective energy, there was a more mundane reason why being observed enabled the martyr to fulfill the role expectation successfully. Knowing that the group was watching exercised a restraining influence on the tendency to recant. A recanting martyr-designate would ever after have to live with the personal defeat of failing to live up to expectations. Martyrdom was essentially a local behavior, and the martyr-designates were in the company of their local communion, observed by its members and accompanied by them throughout.

As Riddle indicates, "another aspect of the influence of the group is apparently the lesson learned by the Christian leaders that successful examples of martyrdom were salutary only when accomplished in the martyr's home surrounding. It was found that when death occurred elsewhere, the loss of effect upon the Christians was serious."[21] Thus, being observed by those one knew and trusted was a strong factor in encouraging the martyrological response. Canonization of martyrs tended to be sponsored by locals who sought the support of regional and national groups and who finally petitioned the Church as a whole. In a word, successful martyrdom was heavily dependent on a local venue, observation, memorialization and promotion.

---

[21]Riddle, ibid, p. 88.

4. Programmed for emotions and demeanor

What is important in assessing the various means used by the early church to encourage martyrdom is to appreciate the all embracing nature of the means that were used. It was not only external behavior that was controlled through promise and threat, but it was also inner disposition and attitude. In fact one might say that in the control of attitude, judging from the reports that have come down to us, the Church made the most remarkable progress.

The Predisposition Towards Martyrdom

We will now turn to a central question in any analysis of the martyr's motive: what is more significant in sustaining the martyr's motive – the power of the cause or an inner predisposition towards martyrdom and self sacrifice? It is interesting to note that, in a discussion about martyrdom, most people have already predecided this issue one way or the other. Since our discussion has centered principally on the sociological aspects of the martyr's motive, we will now attempt to analyze the phenomenon of predisposition through a study of one of the most famous Jewish-Christian martyrs of modern times – Simone Weil.

Martyrdom can be more than a one-time act. It can be a way of being in the world, an attitude towards reality which has antecedents in the personal biography of the martyr. The documentation of these previous tendencies is generally done after the martyr has died and his or her fame has spread. In the case of Simone Weil, a Jewess who embraced Christian theology, there is ample testimony to the various antecedents of the final act.

Simone Weil died as a martyr through self-imposed starvation in 1943. She left an unforgettable record of her predisposition towards martyrdom in the form of writings and conversations with friends. From these documents it appears that her tendency towards self sacrifice was clearly more influential and relevant in her subsequent martyrdom than the power of her cause.[22] The cause for which she died was spiritualized and ethereal, and to this day remains somewhat obscure. As Father Thibon, one of her spiritual mentors commented, "I had the impression of being in the presence of an absolutely transparent soul that was ready to be reabsorbed into original light."[23] It appears that she sacrificed herself for the "original light."

---

[22]The same apparently holds true for Vincent Van Gogh, according to the interpretation by Lubin, A.J. *The Life of Vincent Van Gogh – Stranger on Earth* (1975).

[23]Petrerent S., *Simone Weil, A Life* (1976), p. 463.

However, the obscurity of her cause does not detract from the awesomeness of her martyrological sacrifice in the eyes of her coterie of admirers. Her motives were felt to be pure and her actions full of integrity. As one of her biographers has noted, "Nobody has more heroically endeavored to bring her actions into accord with her ideas."[24]

Her ideas can best be understood through the stories she cherished. One of her favorites was Grimm's Fairy Tale of the Six Swans. In this story a wicked witch transforms her six sons-in-law into swans. In order to redeem them, their sister must spin and sew six nightshirts for them out of white anemones. During the six years it takes her to spin and sew, she is forbidden to speak. Her silence makes others misconstrue her motives and she is sentenced to die at the gallows. She manages, however, to finish the shirts in time. After throwing them over the swans, thereby returning them to human form, she is vindicated.

Weil's comments on the story are revealing. "To make six shirts from anemones and to keep silent: this is our only way of acquiring power ... Whoever spends six years sewing white anemones cannot be distracted by anything; they are perfectly pure flowers; but above all anemones are almost impossible to sew into shirts, and this difficulty prevents any other action from altering the purity of the six year silence. The sole strength in the world is purity; all that which is without admixture is a fragment of the truth. Never have iridescent silks been worth as much as a beautiful diamond ... The sole strength and sole virtue is to cease from acting ..."[25]

Simone Weil was fascinated with the theme of imprisoned embodiment and the need to fashion a new skin. A skin more pure than the one she was endowed with. As one of her friends commented, "she looked forward with a kind of joy to being delivered from herself."[26]

Another story she treasured was that of Alexander in the desert. While crossing a stretch of desert with his men, a cask of water was brought at great inconvenience so that he could slake his thirst. On receiving the cask he proceeded to pour its content out onto the sand. As Weil comments: "Nobody, much less Alexander, would have dared predict this astonishing deed; but once the deed is accomplished there is nobody who does not have the feeling that it had to be like this ..." For Weil, had Alexander drunk the water he would have caused an unacceptable separation between his own state of being and that of his men. Only by sharing their thirsty plight did he have the moral right

---

[24]Ibid, p. VIII.
[25]Ibid, p. 36.
[26]Ibid, p. 528.

to leadership. As she indicates "Sacrifice is the acceptance of pain, the refusal to obey the animal in oneself, and the will to redeem suffering men through voluntary suffering. Every saint has poured out the water; every saint has rejected all well-being that would separate him from the suffering of men ..."[27]

Weil not only needed to suffer with those around her who were in pain, but prepared herself for a greater pain, which would be a redemptive pain that saves others. As she wrote, "It is quite possible that one day we will be tortured. So we should prepare ourselves for it."[28] She expressed these sentiments in her admiration for Malraux's character Katov in the book "Man's Fate." He "decides to be burnt alive and die, not in order to be annihilated but to save two of his comrades from the same death."[29] She was attracted to dangerous situations and longed for them. "I want to be truly useful. I want to go wherever there is the greatest danger ... where my life will be the least protected."[30] While in New York City during the occupation of France, she decided to eat very little because the French had little food to eat. She said to her parents, "I will not eat more than in Marseilles."[31]

These ideas culminated in her concept of decreation, i.e. "To make something created pass into uncreated."[32] Essentially, what Weil means is that we should empty ourselves of all false divinity with which we were born. Thus, "Once we have understood we are nothing, the object of all our efforts is to become nothing. It is for this that we suffer with resignation, *it is for this that we act,* it is for this that we pray. May God grant that I become nothing. In so far as I become nothing, God loves Himself through me."[33]

These sentiments are similar to those uttered by Ignatius of Antioch: "I am God's wheat and I am ground by the teeth of wild beasts that I may be found pure bread ... Then shall I be truly a disciple of Jesus Christ, when the world shall not so much as see my body." Towards the end of Simone Weil's life she was reported to have said to a friend, "You are like me, a badly cut-off piece of God. But soon I will no longer be cut-off; I will be united and reattached."[34] Upon her death

---

[27]Ibid, p. 37.
[28]Ibid, p. 175.
[29]Ibid, p. 210.
[30]Ibid, p. 455.
[31]Ibid, p. 527.
[32]Panichas, G.A., *The Simone Weil Reader* (1977), p. 350.
[33]Ibid, p. 352.
[34]Petrerent S., *Simone Weil*, p. 528.

by starvation, the headline in the Southeastern English Gazetteer read, "Death from Starvation – French Professor's Curious Sacrifice."[35]

Weil's martyrological predisposition was thus a mixture of the following diverse factors:

1.   An ethereal cause,
2.   A fanatic insistence on integrity (the congruence of attitude and behavior),
3.   An unwillingness to be separated from the suffering of others,
4.   A fascination with danger,
5.   The sense of an imprisoned embodiment,
6.   A yearning for delivery from the self,
7.   A belief in the redemption of the suffering of other through a voluntary act,
8.   An anticipation of greater pain.

If all these factors do not constitute a predisposition towards martyrdom, than nothing does. In Weil's writings one finds a well developed martyr's motive for a spiritual ineffable cause.

The Martyr's Motive and the Power of the Cause

It is not only people with a general predisposition towards martyrdom who become martyrs. There are also people who find themselves willing to die for a particular powerful cause in which they believe. We will now attempt to trace how causes generate a set of beliefs or convictions.

Most people live in rather limited cognitive worlds. The territory of the known is surrounded by a dark unknown set of undiscovered facts. The same can be said of the emotional inner world of likes and dislikes. In order that something new enter the cognitive and emotional world of an individual, it must first be noticed. This requires considerable effort, as any advertising expert knows. Amidst the vast array of known elements in life, for a new element to stand out requires that it be distinctive and call attention to itself in unusual ways. When it does, it can be with varying degrees of salience.

There are new factors in life which are so prominent that all other known facts are then placed in the shadow. These new elements can become a prism through which everything else is seen and experienced. In profound conversion to a cause, this is what happens. Most powerful causes offer comprehensive ideologies about all that exists, or at least

---

[35]Ibid, p. 537.

purport to do so. At the moment when the individual begins to develop a belief in the cause, there is still a kind of separation between the person and the belief. The movement from belief to conviction relates to the amount of stake a person has in the cause.

To deny a belief is not necessarily to deny oneself, but to deny a conviction is to die a little. There are convictions that grow and develop. As they do so they begin to crowd out what was once an independent person. The cause takes over. It becomes an all for the person, and it is difficult to distinguish the person from the conviction. It is at that point that a need for self-transcendence develops. What is left of an independent self becomes a hindrance. There is a need to prove that the cause *is all*. Such proof is provided through expungement of the corporeal self. It is only when the individual becomes superfluous that the cause becomes all. This is the generative moment when the cause creates martyrs.

As this process is unfolding on the psychological level, a social movement is generally developing with leaders who are seeking to enlist supporters. As we have seen earlier in this chapter, the attention and sympathy of observers must be enlisted, and there must be examples of those with sufficient conviction to legitimize and demonstrate the hold of the cause over people.

For all these reasons, leaders have an interest in the creation of martyrs for their cause. Their work is easier if they find people with martyr-like predispositions. However, some leaders are adept at creating martyrs even out of those without conviction.

We have discussed the impact of the martyrological confrontation and the formulation of conviction through the martyr's motive. In our next chapter we will discuss the creation of martyrs through the conscious manipulation of the martyr narrative.

5

The Martyr Narrative and the Manipulation of Conviction

In the hands of a skilled propagandist, martyrdom and the convictions it represents can be manipulated to attain predetermined aims. The capacity of the martyr to infuse meaning and to inspire commitment can be used by astute leaders to manipulate sentiments and actions during times of stress. In this chapter we will present several dramatic examples of a premeditated fabrication of the martyr myth. First, however, we will touch on the stratagems which make this powerful association possible.

The Unconscious Implanter

In modern advertising it is a commonplace that the good packaging of powerful symbols can reach deeply into the unconscious. An association is then forged between the familiar symbol and the product or idea to be sold.[1] For the purpose of our analysis, we will use the concept of an unconscious implanter to describe this deeply embedded association created by the symbol which is introduced.

A good example of this sequence can be seen in the early Christian martyrology. Potamianena was a martyred woman who was described in the ancient martyrologies in particularly erotic terms. She was a "struggler for the maintenance of her bodily purity. Boundless was the struggle she endured against her lovers in defense of her bodily purity and chastity (in which she was pre-eminent), for the perfection of her body as well as her soul was in full flower."[2] In this description, there is a powerful conjunction of the concepts of body and soul, perfection and

---

[1]c.f. Langholz Leymore, V., *Hidden Myth – Structure and Symbolism in Advertising* (1975).
[2]c.f. Musurillo, H.A., *The Acts of the Christian Martyrs* (1954).

chastity. Everything was in bloom while preserved in purity.

Potamianena is saved from the "assaults" of the gladiators by Basilides, a Christian soldier. He then leads her directly to the execution. She is tortured and killed with "boiling pitch which was slowly poured drop by drop over different parts of her body from her toes to the top of her head."[3]

To Basilides and to many others in Alexandria at the time, the scene of Potamianena's martyrdom proved unforgettable. Three days after her death she appeared to Basilides in a dream and called his name. He is so moved by the experience that he asserts his Christian commitments in a confrontational situation, and is then martyred himself. Potamianena's tortured beauty similarly affected others in Alexandria who were called by her in their dreams, and many new converts were reported to have gone over to the word of Jesus.

This is a powerful example of the seductive appeal of the implanter. A beautiful, pure woman, in full flower, is horribly tortured for her convictions. She addresses men in their sleep, calling them to put on their heads a crown of thorns, and promising to welcome them "before long." This imagery was a far more effective appeal from the early Christian community than that of their system of beliefs and way of life. The narrative of a legitimate martyr reached deeply into the unconscious and forged an association which inspired commitment and renewed conviction.

Martyrdom and the Goals of a Secular Revolution

As we have seen in the origins of martyrology, the recorded early history of martyrdom is associated with religious movements and the conflicts between religious convictions. However, it was not only religious movements which were mobilized by the martyr's lessons in convictions. There was a moment in western history when the radical transformation from religious to secular was made. This transformation basically took place in 1789 at the time of the French Revolution. It was during this high moment in history that the heroic inspiration of the martyr was harnessed to serve the goals of a national, secular movement.

Through references veiled in Christian imagery, martyrdom was consciously and forthrightly used in order to dramatize secular political ideals. The artist David became the arch martyrizer of the French Revolution. He used both his brush and his capacity for creating pageantry to keep the moral passions in France aflame. He highlighted the moral issues of the times, including the plight of

---

[3]Ibid.

families tragically rent by conflicting loyalties, through the romantic depiction of horror and devotion. In many of his pictures, he created an ambience of crypto-Christian martyrdom.

David's painting of Marat's death has been depicted by art historians as "The most powerful symbol of the mixture of both secular and sacred motifs. The clandestine Christian imagery helps to transform a secular to a sacred theme. There is the slaughtered corpse of the thirteen year old drummer boy, Joseph Bara, shot by royalist troops in 1793 when he responded 'Vive la Republique!' to their demand that he proclaim the King."[4]

David's speech on the occasion of Marat's death demonstrates his use of religious martyrological imagery:

> Citizens, the people were again calling for their friend – their desolate voice was heard: 'David! take up your brushes ... avenge Marat' ... 'I heard the voice of the people, I obeyed' ... 'It is to you, my colleagues, that I offer the homage of my brush. Your glances running over the livid and blood stained features of Marat will recall to you his virtues, which must never cease to be your own ... I vote for Marat, the honor of the Pantheon.'[5]

In the initial stages of revolution, art is useful in depicting the ideal. Natural sentiments are suspended in favor of such an ideal. We have met this tendency before in the story of Hannah and her seven sons, and in the early church martyrologies. The love of parents for children, the desire to live, are suspended in favor of devotion to the ideals of the cause. With secular revolutions, these basic sentiments become less important than the ideals of the revolution, and are subservient to political purposes. David, the artist of the French Revolution, dramatizes this point through the portrayal of stoic males with the courage to make difficult "moral" decisions. They are shown in contrast to mourning women, who are lost in their hysteria.

When a cause is in the early stages of transformation from an idea to a social reality, demonstrating devotion to that cause through the killing of children is a particularly strong theme. This theme is stressed by David at the initial stages of the French Revolution, and he went back in history to depict the heroism of earlier fathers, like Brutus, who had martyred their children for a noble, secular cause. The story shown in his painting is that of Lucius Junius Brutus, the founder of the Roman Republic. He was responsible for the death of his sons, Titus

---

[4]Rosenbloom, Exemplum Virtues, p. 84-85.
[5]Dowd, D.L., *Pageant Maker of the Republic, Jacques Louis David and the French Revolution* (1948), p. 107.

and Tiberius, because of their treason in trying to restore the Tarquins to the throne.

It is the men who do the killing for crimes of treason in David's depictions. Virginius kills his daughter, Horatius kills his sister, and Manleus Torquatos kills his son – all for treason to the new Republic. There is, thus, a striking contrast in the depiction of the early Christian women martyrs, who are seen as brave, steadfast and unrelenting in their resolve, and the women of the French Revolution, who are portrayed by David as hopelessly mired in human sentiments. They are not glorified in those paintings which served to inflame the passions of the new French Republic. It is interesting to note that a century later, during the Russian revolution, the theme of killing for treason returned. The Menshivik philosopher, Gregor Plekhanov, praised David's art for its patriotic presentation of a father suppressing normal sentiments in favor of the state's welfare.[6]

It would be a mistake to see this glorification of secular patriotism and of the martyr as an expression of artistic impulse alone. Robespierre in 1792 strongly stressed the importance of martyrs such as Jean Paul Marat. Each martyr was acclaimed, and the daggers, ropes, vials of poison or guillotine blade which were the instruments of their deaths were boldly depicted. Robespierre regarded these martyrs as the great benefactors of mankind. In his proclamations, he placed the revolutionary mayor of Paris, Petion De Villeneuve, in the same category as Cato, Brutus and Jesus.

Like David, the artist of secular martyrdom, Robespierre was aware that "the blood of the martyrs was indeed the seed of the revolutionary faith. He knew that the enthusiasm of the crowd was necessary for the continuation of the revolution, and that the crowd was more easily moved by cults of martyrs for liberty than by such vague abstractions as Reason and Law."[7]

During the French Revolution, the manipulative use of the martyr narrative emerged with great clarity. Such manipulation for secular purposes had been previously unknown; the martyr was used for protection from assassination. Between the Republicans and the Royalists, martyrological narratives were created not only to generate sacred enthusiasm by supporters of the martyr, but to deflect the anger of potential enemies. For instance, a Republican could gain safety from a crowd of Royalists by martyring the assassinated Republican with whom he was identified. Dowd has described this process:

---

[6]Ibid, p. 157.
[7]Rosenbloom, Exemplum Virtues, p. 99.

On the night before Louis' execution, the distinguished deputy, Michel Le Peletier de Saint Fargeu, innocent of fanaticism or violence, had been assassinated by a former royal bodyguard for having voted for the death of the monarch. While they remained calm at the death of their King, many Frenchmen were indignant at the murder of a deputy in the performance of his duties ... Believing themselves threatened with similar violence, Le Peletier's colleagues took measures to protect themselves and arouse public opinion against the royalists by exalting their fellow regicide as a 'martyr of liberty.'

In an address to the French people, the convention announced: 'Citizens, it is not one man alone who has been struck, it is you; it is not Michel Le Peletier who has been basely assassinated, it is you; it is not against the life of a deputy that the blow has been dealt, but against the life of the nation, against public liberty, against public sovereignty.'

David was called upon to organize a state funeral which should drive this point home. In the naked corpse exposed in the Place Vendome and escorted to its last meeting place in the Pantheon, the people saw themselves and were inspired by mingled fury and determination. The death of a King was forgotten in the horror produced by the threat to their own safety and that of the nation. According to all the press accounts, this classically inspired and majestically executed ceremony produced a profoundly moving impression upon the huge crowds which witnessed it. The lucid symbolism of bloody sword and colossal fates was not lost. Frenchmen must unite against the foe or meet the fate of Le Peletier.[8]

As with many other aspects of the modern world, the manipulation of the martyr narrative for secular purposes was clearly launched during the years of the French Revolution. We will now move from France to Germany, and will analyze the significant role of the martyr narrative and its manipulation in German culture.

Goethe's Iphigenia

Martyrs have played an important role in the political and cultural life of Germany for many centuries. It was customary for desirable purposes of all kinds to be linked with the death of martyrs, and one can find in German martyrologies the full range of convictions, from the most narrow chauvinism to the most expansive universalism.

It was Goethe, the German poet, scientist, statesman, critic and universal man of the eighteenth and nineteenth century, who used the martyr narrative to convey the message of man's capacity to rise above the particular. He chose the medium of the Greek martyr Iphigenia, and created a narrative which was wholly different from the original Greek tragedy. In Goethe's play, Iphigenia appeals to the highest moral powers through the acceptance of her doom, and forbids an

---

[8]Dowd, op. cit., p. 100.

appeal to violence even in a just cause. Her new morality of universal trust and love resolves the dangerous situation which her people face.[9]

In the original Greek story of Iphigenia, as recounted in the Iliad, her martyrdom is directed not towards humanity, but to save Hellas, the pride of Greek culture.

Iphigenia, Agamemnon's daughter and a descendent of the ill fated family of Artreus, is offered up as a sacrifice to appease the Goddess Artemis who had becalmed the Archean fleet at Aulis. Due to lack of wind, the ships could not sail for Troy, and Agamemnon's men got restless. The whole expedition to Troy was in danger of dissolving amidst angry discord. It was the sacrifice of Iphigenia which satisfied the Goddess Artemis, and she caused the winds to blow again so that the fleet could set sail. Euripides, the Greek playwright, wrote two plays about Iphigenia based on this ancient legend. In both she emerged as the very model of martyrological devotion to the cause of Hellas.

According to Euripides, Agamemnon convinced his wife Clytemnestra to bring Iphigenia with her to meet him using the pretext that she was to be married to Achilles, one of his warriors. His real intention, however, was to sacrifice her in order to appease the angry Goddess. Iphigenia is depicted as the very epitome of a joyous, expectant bride and dutiful daughter. She arrived in her father's court filled with love and homage for her father. "O mother blame me not! Let me go first and put my arms about my father's neck."[10]

Upon being apprised of her fate, she begs for mercy. "O, kill me not untimely! The sun is sweet! Why will you send me into the dark grave?"[11] She overcomes her fear and sorrow at her fate, summons up the courage to meet her death which is for the service of her beloved Hellas, and gives voice to sentiments which have remained classic utterances for martyrs ever since:

> I have been thinking, mother, hear me now!
> I have chosen death! It is my own free choice.
> I have put cowardice away from me.
>
> Honor is mine now, O, mother say I am right!
> Our country – think – our Hellas – looks to me,
> Our women's honor all the years to come.
> My death will save them, my name be blest,
> She who freed Hellas! Life is not so sweet
> I should be craven. You who bore your child

[9]Treveleyan, H., *Goethe and the Greeks* (1972).
[10]Homer, *The Iliad*, p. 303.
[11]Euripides, Iphigenia, p. 333.

It was for Greece you bore her, not yourself,
Think! Thousands of our soldiers stand to arms,
Ten thousand man the ships, and all on fire
To serve their outraged country, die for Greece,

And is my one poor life to hinder all?
Could we defend that? Could we call it just?
And mother, think! How could we let our friend
Die for a woman, fighting all his folk?
A thousand women are not worth one man!
The Goddess needs my blood. Can I refuse?
No: take it, conquer Troy. This shall be
My husband, and my children, and my fame.
Victory, mother, victory for the Greeks!
The foreigner must never rule this land,
Our own land, They are slaves and we are free!

Follow me now, the victor,
Follow the taker of Troy!
Crown my head with a garland ...

Leader of the Chorus
Ah, your glory will not die ...
Behold!
Behold the conqueror of Troy!
She is crowned and made pure for a goddess' joy.
She goes to the dead.
Her white neck pierced, her blood running red ...[12]

This version of Iphigenia at Tauris was used by Goethe to illustrate principles which were very different from those of Euripides. In Euripides' version the solution to Orestes problem and Iphigenia's fate is external and coercive. It is based on the power and might of the Greeks. Not so in Goethe's version. According to Goethe, Iphigenia is able to arouse reactions that are universal and valid even in the breast of the non-Greek King. This allows her and her brother to escape his evil decree. Her faith in his humanity is dramatically portrayed in the following scene:

---

[12]Euripides, Iphigenia, p. 329-330.

Thoas [13]

> And dost thou think
> That the uncultured Scythian will attend
> The voice of truth and humanity
> which Atreus, the Greek, heard not?

Iphigenia

> 'Tis heard
> By everyone born 'neath whatever clime,
> Within whose bosom flows the stream of life,
> Pure and unhindered. What thy thought? O King!
> What silent purpose broods in thy deep soul?...
> Look on us, King! an opportunity
> For such noble deed not oft occurs.
> Refuse thou canst not, – give thy quick consent.

Thoas
> Then go!

Goethe's manipulation of the martyr narrative was in the interests of imparting a lesson in cosmopolitanism. We will now turn, however, to a manipulation of the martyr narrative which was expressly designed to serve a very different set of purposes.

Martyrdom and the Nazi Party

It was Joseph Goebbels, the chief propagandist for the Nazi party, who exploited the potency of the martyr symbol under very differing circumstances. Goebbels' successful manipulations had an impact not only on the German people during the Nazi regime, but on the subsequent perception of martyrdom and of zealous conviction in the western world. We will now consider in greater detail the malleability of the martyr narrative in the hands of this master craftsman.

Goebbels' martyr, Horst Wessel, represents to most people, the essence of perversity, a fabricated reduction to the lowest common denominator of the basest of human sentiments; while Goethe's martyr, Iphigenia in Tauris, is generally regarded as one of the most sublime examples of the transcending of ethnocentric loyalties. Both, in our view, are works of genius.

Gordon Craig writes about an experience in the late 1930's. When riding in a public bus in Berlin he passed the Feldherrnhalle where Residenzstrasse empties into Odeonplatz. On the site was a plaque

---

[13]Goethe, J.W. *Iphigenia in Tauris* (1902), Acts, Scene 3. pp. 81-82, p. 90.

commemorating twelve conspirators in the abortive 1923 Putsch who had been killed and celebrated as martyrs for the Nazi cause. In describing the experience he writes that he felt the bus virtually lift off the pavement as the arms of passengers were "sweeping up in dedicated unison" in homage to the dead martyrs using the salute of the Hitler Gruss. The German people loved and respected martyrs and responded to their memory with subservient devotion.[14]

Hitler knew this and, in the opening passages of Mein Kampf, he chose to describe his own birthplace reverently as "The little town on the Inn, hallowed by German martyrdom." In addition to this association with his physical origins Hitler very much wanted the German people to believe that his political awakening and resolve to change the face of Germany originated in the throes of a martyr's agony. According to a widely circulated, early authorized biography, he is described as the pathetic sufferer for all the humiliations of defeated Germany in World War I.

The following depiction was prefixed to a volume of his speeches which appeared shortly before the Putsch. It purportedly describes his condition as a patient when being treated for eye injuries (as well as psychological symptoms) at Pasewalk Infirmary in November 1918, due to a gas attack on the front.

> A solitary bed stands in a darkened room. A nurse lays cooling bandages on the patient's eyes. He starts in fright. Drunken squalling, sounds ceaselessly from the barracks where sons of Pomerania once were raised to proud manliness. Kings dragoons, victors of Hohenfriedberg, victors of a thousand battles of Prussian-German history, bodyguards of her Majesty the German Empress!
>
> The nurse's arms support the tortured one, who sits upright. She wants to push him back down onto the pillows, this uncanny patient brought there blinded and muted – how does his record read? – ...'private first class, disabled in enemy gas attack.' She knows no more about him. Yet she sees the ineffable suffering of this semicorpse whose facial expressions and whose gestures into the distance indicate more and more distinctly from day to day that he knows that something frightful has broken upon Germany! None of the degrading news from Kiel, Munich, and now from red Berlin has penetrated this solitary ward.
>
> And yet – the sister reads it from the martyred countenance: 'Not my own suffering, the catastrophe that felled me, not that I am never to behold the sun or starry heavens or-my homeland, but what is happening out there that I hear, feel-see! That is insufferable torment! My Germany!'

---

[14]Craig, G.A. *The Germans* (1982).

> The nurse holds the twitching, feverish soldier of the betrayed
> army in her arms ...

In this account of Hitler's supposed martyrdom the reader is
virtually begged on bended knees to conjure up the image of
Michelangelo's Pieta. The image is served up with a strong dose of
melodramatic kitsch, a characteristic of virtually all of Nazi
propaganda. Hitler is portrayed as the one who suffers, through his
physical infirmities, all the indignities of his "beloved Germany" in
its fallen condition. Through his martyred condition he is the
personification, the very anthropomorphization of the suffering of the
body politic. But the martyrdom is only a prelude. We are quickly
reassured that out of this pathos-filled condition something is about to
happen which will have a great impact on Germany's future. A
veritable Christ like figure rising from the grave.

> ...a higher constraint brings good words to her lips, words of faith in
> Germany's resurrection. And a miracle comes to pass. He who was
> consecrated to eternal night, who had suffered through his Golgotha
> in this hour, spiritual and bodily crucifixion, pitiless death as on the
> cross, with senses keen, one of the lowliest out of the mighty host of
> broken heroes-he becomes seeing! The spasms of his features
> subside. And in an ecstasy peculiar to the dying seer, new light fills his
> dead eyes, new radiance, new life!
>
> A disarmed warrior was brought, mute and blinded, to the
> infirmary in the Pomeranian village. An upstanding fighter strides out
> into the alienized German world. He is armed to the teeth with faith,
> will and confidence in victory! Invincible weapons![15]

Such transparent self-serving pap was the very stuff of Nazi
propaganda.

Because of its symbolic power in Germany, it was not only the
fascists who had recourse to martyrdom. In one of the most publicized
trials of the period the artist George Grosz used the image of Jesus on
the cross to emphasize his anti-war sentiments. In the drawing "Christ
With a Gas Mask," Jesus is shown crucified on the cross wearing a gas
mask and a pair of boots similar to those issued to soldiers at the front
during the first World War. Underneath is a caption, "Shut Up and Do
Your Duty." When asked in court to explain its meaning Grosz indicated
that, had Christ come into the trenches during the War, bearing the
messages of love and brotherhood, he would have been issued boots and
a gas mask and told to shut up. Upon refusing, Christ would have been
crucified again.

---

[15]Quote from Binion, R., *Hitler Among the Germans* (1976), pp. 137-138.

In December, 1928 Grosz and his publisher came to trial in Charlottenburg-Berlin and were declared guilty of a blasphemous offense against the Church and Christ. He and his publisher Herzfelde were fined 2,000 marks instead of serving two months in prison. They appealed the decision and the judgement was reversed a few months later. But the uproar among the Conservatives was horrendous. Questions were raised about the case in the Prussian parliament and the presiding Judge Landgerichtsdirektor Siegert was one of the first judges dismissed by the Nazi regime when it came to power.[16] The martyr figure was to be reserved for their own use.

While these uses of martyrdom had varying degrees of success as political propaganda, it can be said with certainty that Joseph Goebbels was the most successful modern fabricator of martyrs, and a master in their premeditated, cynical use. He, as few before him, successfully managed to create and use martyrs in order to arouse and empassion Nazi convictions among the German masses. He managed to turn the martyr into a symbol of mass persecution that had powerful political effects. The passions aroused at the mass rallies that he staged, which contributed in no small measure to Hitler's success, were very much dependent on the atmosphere of reverential dedication and infectious conviction that was generated by rituals celebrating martyrs. Most Nazi meetings began with some reference to Nazi martyrs, either in ritual, song or speech. In fact, as we already begin to suspect, the Nazis were fairly well obsessed with martyrs.

But no one more than Goebbels. He was a skillful and dedicated propagandist. His search for the perfect martyr, and the cynical, yet effective exploitation of the martyr's story for political means, bears telling in detail. Only through a detailed description of the fabrication process can one see the full power and effectiveness of the martyr's suggestive symbolism and its function as a contagious symbol of conviction.

We might first question, however, of what possible interest are the Nazi fictions to us, more than sixty years after the fact? The response to this question, in our view, is that the successful placement of these martyrological fictions in the collective psyche of a cultured nation helped to inspire, embolden, justify and glorify acts of horror, the likes of which have rarely been equaled on the face of the earth. Not a trifling matter. It seems that lies have quotients of potency. They do varying degrees of damage. There are lies; then there are lies that help to change the course of history. What interests us is the manner in

---

[16]Lewis, B.L., *George Grosz: Art and Politics in the Weimar Republic* (1971), pp. 218-223.

which the particularly effective martyrological fictions created by Goebbels gained their power over the mind of Germany. What was it about them that proved so effective? In short, we wish to understand the mysterious process whereby the fictitious, fabricated version of one person's death, becomes the basis of conviction for the masses. How does this come about?

Goebbels' Search for the Perfect Martyr: Trial and Error

On March 14 1923, a young man by the name of Albert Schlageter participated in a sabotage scheme near Dusseldorf which was designed to harass the French in the occupied zone. He, together with a small group of men stationed at Essen, blew up a section of the railroad track between Dusseldorf and Duisburg. He was apprehended and jailed. Under interrogation, he confessed his part in the sabotage raid and implicated his fellow plotters, revealing the names of prominent German industrialists who had given support to the budding German Nationalist movement. The industrialists included Gustav Krupp and Fritz Thyssen. As a result of these revelations the German government was forced to resign. They were succeeded in office by a government which changed the policy of passive resistance to the occupation.[17]

In his propaganda campaign, Goebbels decided to disregard the fact that Schlageter had dishonorably precipitated a serious crisis in the movement by revealing the details of the resistance activities. Instead, he chose to eulogize Schlageter following his execution on May 26, 1923. As Curt Reiss, Goebbels' biographer has phrased it: "He talked about Schlageter. He did not admit that Schlageter had been a paid agent, who had been guilty of the lowest and most dishonorable act, that of squealing: far from it. While talking he subtly transformed reality and put a legend in its place; he turned an informer into a hero, into an unselfish patriot, a martyr, who preferred to go to his death rather than betray his cause ..."[18] That the facts of the case did not accord with the martyrological depiction, in no way deterred Goebbels. He successfully managed to create the impression that Schlageter had indeed acted as a selfless martyr for the Nazi cause. The description of Schlageter's alleged actions and their meaning to the movement has been preserved in a number of Nazi publications. These were versions that Goebbels had a hand in editing.

A typical one is as follows:[19]

---

[17]Reiss, C. *Joseph Goebbels: A Biography* (1948).
[18]Reiss, C. Ibid.
[19]The Nazi propaganda brochures on Nazi Martyrs were obtained from the Wiener Library in London; translation from German our own.

Hoist the Flag
Albert Leo Schlageter
Essen, March, 1923

The greatest violating outrage of a treaty of all time was a fact. French and Belgians had occupied the area of the river Ruhr. In the middle of peace, so called peace, in a quiet location, several men sat together and talked in low voices. In the streets the French dominated the scene, officers walked on the sidewalks and would hit many men or women in their faces if they would not step aside quickly enough. The shame burnt, burnt, with an intensity that was inextinguishable. 'Something has to be done', said a slim and relatively young man, who had sharp features and alert penetrating eyes.

'It can't go on like this. Not like this!' The population was forced to be silent. But there was protest nonetheless. Shopkeepers closed their shops, no hotel or pension accepted voluntarily French clientele. What was the response of the French to this?

By force they evicted people from their beds in the middle of the night. They did this by force and brutal oppression.

Albert Schlageter hit his fist on the table and looked at his comrades ... 'Did we not fight in the Baltic States, rap the knuckles of the Poles...'

The martyrological version continues with the recounting of his various war exploits and ends with a description of his last day.

Be Loyal Until Death

Schlageter sat in his cell, well composed, he had fully withdrawn from life, from everyone. He wrote nonetheless a last touching letter to his parents:

'Dear Mother, Dear Father,

My heart seems to break by the thought what terrible pain and sadness this letter will cause you. It will remain my deepest wish till the last hour, that our good God will give you the strength and consolation to endure these difficult hours. If it would be possible somehow I beg you to write me a few lines. It would give me strength on my last journey. Now live well. I kiss and embrace you in my thoughts once more.

Albert'

A puppet in the political game that required a sacrifice! And he was that sacrifice. A conscious person till his death. He had neither wishes nor hopes. Berlin was powerless. He was sacrificed to the French Moloch. How gladly would he have given his life if there would have been the tiniest hope for Germany, but they (the French) would shoot him like a defenseless dog. And the Ruhr area would still remain occupied. That was the most bitter part, which made death so difficult to accept for him.

At 12:30 after midnight, the order arrived in Dusseldorf, signed by Poincare. Schlageter wasn't sleeping, he was writing in his cell. It was terribly quiet in the corridors. Suddenly-2:00 A.M., the sound of rattling keys. The door of the cell was opened. A French officer informed him that the verdict would be executed.

'Do you have any last wishes?'

'I would only like to write some lines to my parents.' Which he was permitted to do. With a steady and clear hand he wrote to them. A Clergyman entered the cell.

The French officer, nonetheless chooses to remain. At which point Schlageter says: 'I refuse to talk with God in the presence of soldiers.' The clergyman talked softly with the officer. He was allowed five minutes for the Holy Communion. Then still one question after the last wish.

'A cigarette?'

He thought to himself, only not to lose one's nerves, and said, 'Not right now'...be brave, like Andreas Hofer,[20] like all those already before him who had stood in front of the French guns. He cast a last look at the small calendar, which he had made during his imprisonment from the cover of a cigarette box. (The picture of the box itself is shown in the version). The 25th of May, – he had noted the day before without realizing that he had marked the end of his life. Now it was the 26th of May. Now they came for him. Now they came for him, when everything would be over.

Germany! Nobody saved him. But still, Germany!

It was his last and deep belief.

Daylight is breaking, the sky is colored red, the candidate for death enters the car which is bound for the Horsheimer heath. He enters without hesitation ... one moment he seems to falter, then he says quietly and clear, 'Auf Wiedersehen.'"

"Where is that 'Wiedersehen' in a better country? Schlageter is a pious Christian, a true German. No, they will not see any weakness in him. He is led to the execution place. He is standing on German soil.

A French soldier tells him to kneel down. Schlageter's eyes are flashing, they already seem to belong to another world.

'To kneel down ... no, Never!'

Then the sergeant pushes him in the back of his knees from behind ... and Schlageter sinks to the floor. And ... the German men stand there in silence, they have to keep silent.

The hands of the convicted are bound together from behind. It was totally unnecessary to do this. In fact, it was unheard of behavior on the part of the French to do this. The eyes of the 'convict' were

---

[20]Andreas Hofer (1767-1810) was a native of Tyrol, an Austrian German national hero and a martyr in the struggle against Napoleon. The Nazis had used Hofer as a symbol of sacrifice and resistance and supported the Andreas Hofer league.

flashing contempt, endless contempt for his enemies. As a result even
the officer became restless. It was a most unpleasant matter. It should
be over fast.

'Get back', he orders.

The sound of the drums, the presentation of the company. At the
fringe of the heath stands a lonely farmer with his cart, he is watching
the scene and biting his lips to the point where blood started to flow.
'Something like this is happening in the middle of Germany? In peace
time?' He spits contemptuously, for he has a bitter taste in his mouth.
'To the devil with this...'

The sound of the drums grows softer. Then the prisoner stands up
again. 'No, I will not kneel down ...' The guns are directed at his chest.
A sharp order rings out. 'Fire!'

The sound of a salvo is heard, the unfortunate Schlageter's body is
broken. The adjutant officer puts a revolver to his temple. The last
shot. The poor body straightens up once more and then falls again.

The first soldier of the Third Reich has died. Shot by French
bullets. In his own country.

But now that Schlageter is no more, now there is commotion
abroad in the country. While alive he couldn't be saved. Dead, he has
been transfigured and made into a hero. His comrades obtained his
body from the French and conducted it on a triumphal tour.

Wherever the coffin arrived, every place there were thousands of
people standing at the station, men took off their hats, women were
crying, girls and men stood wiping their tears.

He died for us, so we can live. He remained faithful until death.
Yes, the banner must be kept up, even when the man has fallen! The
death of Schlageter had made the people aware of this fundamental
truth. Like a wave this awareness swept suddenly over Germany. He
has been buried at the foot of his beloved mountains ... and a suitable
monument was erected. Poets sang about him, and he continued to
live in the hearts of the people, as the great sacrifice for the coming of
the state, for the Third Reich. Above his grave the flags of the New
Germany were waving, and they waved and remained even when the
man had fallen.

*Germany has woken up, it is honoring its dead. Schlageter died, so
that we could live.*

What became a glorious reality on the 30th of January, 1933 had
been tried ten years previously by nearly the same men. The national
stirrings in November 1923 shattered the indecisiveness of men who
had given their word and then broken it.

Adolph Hitler had already wanted in 1923 a new Germany. His
movement broke down under the bullets of his own compatriots. But
the battle of the Feldherrnhalle was the beginning of all that was to
come. Out of the bloodbath of that gray day in November, like a
phoenix, rose the holy banner of waking Germany. Therefore men of
letters cannot by-pass or ignore this fundamental historical event.

In this version of Schlageter's death we find many of the familiar devices of the martyrological account. The whole version is an unabashed call for the mobilization of national consciousness: "Hoist the Flag." It is not only Schlageter that is effected. The German people have been insulted. In the streets: they cannot even walk without being required to step aside; in their beds: there is no possibility of secure uninterrupted repose, for they cannot decide who is to sleep where. Their sacred spaces have been invaded. It is not only the Ruhr and German soil, places which are public, – but private space is not safe as well. The effects are created without great subtlety. It is the ultimate shame that the execution takes place on German soil. That shame *requires* a release in action.

But Schlageter's death failed to have the widespread effects that Goebbels wanted. There was something unsatisfying about the version of Schlageter's death as a martyr. It didn't quite come off properly. It lacked some of the necessary ingredients for a good martyrological version. Goebbels did not yet have his prototypical Nazi martyr.

Schlageter's death did not work as martyrdom because his agony was too fleeting; his oppressors were not sufficiently personified (they remain faceless); the cause he died for was not espoused with sufficiently explicit uncompromising zeal; the temptations to forego his cause are not seductive enough; his confrontations with the authorities are pathetic rather than convincingly heroic. Schlageter lacked the infectious appeal that martyrs generate. He does not manage to rise above natural sentiments, such as love for parents. His dedication to the cause did not succeed in demonstrating the transcendence of his principle over all things. Schlageter simply evinces the commonplace consideration of a son for his loving parents. Nice, praiseworthy – but not the stuff of martyrdom.

Furthermore, Schlageter is not an active agent at all stages of the enfolding of his fate. While his resolve motivated him to act initially, his end is dictated by events not of his own making. He bears up well, but he is not the creator of his action. He suffers it more than he generates it. In addition, his hope for ultimate vindication is, for him, subjectively uncertain. "And the Ruhr area would still remain occupied. That was the most bitter part, which made death so difficult to accept for him." This sentiment is far from the conviction of "certain vindication" that characterizes noteworthy martyrs. Hannah's sons, even in the midst of the most excruciating torture could summon up sufficient conviction to actually threaten their tormentors with punishments at some future time. Their own belief in their ultimate vindication was palpable. None of that here.

However, this first version is not totally remote from the typical martyrological sequence of events. Goebbels, the creator of the narrative, shows an understanding of the need to depict a partially faltering resolve at the end, thereby making Schlageter more human. "He thought to himself, only not to lose one's nerves..." In addition, pointing attention to the exact time of the martyrdom demonstrates a sensitivity to the need for clearly marking the fateful day as the possible future anniversary of a celebration. Martyrs and calendars have been intimately connected, certainly in the Christian tradition, in which virtually every day is known by its martyr. The pathetic calendar on the box of matches seems to say that time must forever stand still. The flame of life is to be snuffed out, but the record of its anxious accounting is to be preserved on the container which held those incendiary objects that symbolically created it. How fitting! Too fitting. And lest the reader miss the point, there is a picture of the calendar in the commemorative booklet.

One of the central issues in most martyrological versions is the depiction of the impact of the events not only on sympathetic outsiders, but on the course of subsequent events, and sometimes on nature itself. By explicitly showing the impact of the events on onlookers the narrator is suggesting appropriate reactions to the story on the part of those that are reading it or hearing it for the first time. Here, in Schlageter's case, predictably, the outsider is a prototypical German peasant. His reaction to the sight of the martyrdom is self-inflicted injury, induced by the shame he feels at what he sees.

But it is not only the blood in the mouth of the peasant which is bitter. Nature itself is bloodied by the act in the reddened sky of morning. The bystander, indeed nature itself, suffers with the martyr. Victimhood is generalized to the uttermost degree possible. For the martyr's agony ripples outward and encompasses all and everything in one all- encompassing wave. Everything is similarly victimized by the enormity of the injustice. There can be nothing left unaffected. The effects intended by the martyrologist were, however, not the effects produced in the audiences. Nature could not really be imagined to be recoiling in horror at the events described, and Schlageter's death did not generate in the German people the shame that Goebbels prescribed.

Thus, while Goebbels could transform Schlageter's morally questionable deeds into a kind of retrospective triumph of sorts, those deeds, even with the help of an extravagant melodramatic narrative, could not make a martyr of him. He lacked the infectious appeal that martyrs generate.

Goebbels was to try many times again to find the perfect martyr. One such attempt was the death of Hans Georg Kuetemeyer.

Kuetemeyer, subsequent to his release from the army, became a Nazi sympathizer who did occasional work for the party. One evening, following a speech by Hitler in the Sportpalast, he had gotten drunk. The following morning the police found his body in the Landwehr canal. They discovered a letter he had written indicating that he was fed up with the life of poverty and despaired of finding a job. While the police were fairly certain it was a routine suicide, Goebbels didn't choose to see it that way. Instead he used the occasion to write a number of articles, trying to transform Kuetemeyer into a martyr for the Nazi cause.

Kuetemeyer, according to the Goebbels account, loved the party and existed for it alone. He was swept away by the events at the Sportspalast, especially when he heard the Fuehrer's speech. He sat with his comrades, drinking to be sure, but the drinking was as a result of an emotional high related to the "great events of the evening." According to Goebbels, Kuetemeyer, upon leaving his comrades, was viciously attacked by a group of Communist thugs. He allegedly was smashed with iron bars, knocked unconscious and thrown into the canal. Unlike the police, Goebbels knew precisely when the murder took place; "At four in the morning his wife awakened. She was sure she had heard her husband call 'Mother, Mother!' That was the hour when he died." As Curt Reiss, Goebbels' biographer has written: "Goebbels did his utmost to build up the dead Kuetemeyer. He proclaimed that Kuetemeyer's name would be carried on the honor roll of Party Members who had died for the cause. He would be remembered along with the victims of Hitler's cause, along with Schlageter. But it was in vain. The Kuetemeyer story just did not come off. Soon he was completely forgotten."[21]

The Horst Wessel Legend

For Goebbels, the unsuccessful attempts at creating a Nazi martyr were a prelude to the grand achievement of the Horst Wessel legend. It was through the Wessel legend that Goebbels provided the German people with the hero he believed they wanted – and that he needed, to manipulate them more effectively. A hero they indeed took to their hearts. And in an ironic way, as we shall see subsequently, Wessel was a hero they fully deserved.

The best known aspect of the Horst Wessel martyrdom, was the song that became the Nazi Party anthem. Wessel, who was born in 1907 and was killed in 1930, had written a short poem shortly before he died. It was found to fit a popular melody and Goebbels arranged to

---

[21]Reiss, C., op. cit., p. 60-61.

have it sung as a threnody at Wessel's funeral. The poem went as follows:

Hoist the flag, the ranks are tightly closed,
The S.A. is marching quiet and steady
The spirit of the comrades, killed at the Red front
    and in the Reaction
Are marching with us in our ranks.

Make room for the Brown Battalion
Make room for the Sturmabteilungsmann
Already millions are watching the swastika, filled
    with hope,
The day of freedom and bread has come.

For the last time the roll is called.
All of us are ready for the battle,
Soon the Hitler flag will be hung out in every street.
Slavery will be over soon.

Hoist the flag...etc...[22]

This song was sung by millions, on thousands of occasions during the Third Reich, and immediately before it came to power. It had a hypnotizing effect on vast audiences and was especially effective with the very young. The effect of the song was connected with the fabrication of the Horst Wessel myth. As we shall now see, Goebbels fabricated the myth differently to suit various audiences. It was constructed to convey meanings and lessons that he felt were of service to the Nazi cause. In its various versions, Wessel's martyrdom became a kind of all-purpose carrier of Nazi truth. We will study first the various versions presented to the people before we look into what "really" happened to the man.

Horst Wessel; Poet, Lyricist and Composer

In the following depiction, Wessel is presented as a product of the nationalistic religious tradition. It was in Passewalk, the very site of Hitler's martyrdom, epiphany and resurrection, that Wessel, too, has a "baptism of fire." There he presumably emerges as a leader "caught up in the rhythm of the songs that he sang enthusiastically." Songs that embodied the spirit of the new radicalism on behalf of Germany. Above all else his love of nature and of his country is stressed. It is a love that is informed by youthful enthusiasm. He is both poet, lyricist and

---

[22]Translation our own.

natural leader, the archetype of the activistic invincible hero. He could venture into the very heart of enemy territory and, nonetheless, by the sheer force of his conviction and the magical impact of his personality could manage to escape unscathed.

According to the Goebbels narratives, though he engaged in the most dangerous kinds of activities, Wessel not only inspired his contemporaries, but the old farmers as well (again the farmer spectator!). They are convinced to the point of exclaiming, "these boys are right." This same contagious impact of his conviction holds true "even (for) old experienced fighters from the other camp." They too come over to the Nazi side because of Horst Wessel. He was presented as a bard and a prophet whose song was a battle cry, hammering his message into the hearts of millions; a zealous poet, possessed by an irresistible fire that was destined to purify Germany.

Goebbels's Wessel was the personification of the awakened German spirit's greatness. It may have been a hopelessly melodramatic, one dimensional romantic hero that emerged, but it worked its effects. The gullibility of the admiring public knew no bounds. The following version, presented for public consumption in a Nazi propaganda booklet – Die Fahne Hoch,[23] shows Goebbels's low view of public sensibilities. It was, however, a version which had many avid believers.

> A second Theodor Korner:
>
> At times of downfall and amidst the period of the greatest shame of a nation, there are always men, who by means of the power of their acts and words are able to restore the people's pride and love of being a part of their nation. In the War of Liberation, in 1813, there was Theodor Korner. There was a similarity in the fate of both these two freedom singing heroes.
>
> Theodor Korner was a volunteer of the Lubowshen Freikorps and was killed by a bullet on the 17th of August, 1813 at Gadebush, near Schwerms. Horst Wessel was a member of the S.A. and was shot by the bullets of the 'red murderers.' Both were young and were students and gave all they could to their country. Both died nearly at the same age and both became immortal because of the songs that they created for the people.
>
> As the son of an evangelical minister, Horst Wessel was slated to become a student in the academic world. With the outbreak of the World War his father was a government minister of Kovno in the headquarters of Oberoft. The young Wessel lived through this period, which was one both of great pride as well as enormous suffering for Germany. But he was well aware of the meaning of the shameful peace for Germany.

---

[23]Obtained from the Wiener Library, London, England.

For years he was caught in a conflict of conscience. His heart belonged to his fatherland. He wanted to fight for a better Germany; consequently, he joined various national organizations. He spent his youth near the respectable Nicolai Church at which a certain Paul Gerhard, a great religious poet preached. The spirit of the old and venerable Prussian tradition blew around the house on the Judenstrasse 51/52 ... and by the age of 18 he finished school and began his study of the law.

He was a lover of hiking and got to know his country well ... His temperament led him to become involved in the front lines of the national movement. He craved action. This led to his joining the Scharzen Reichwehs, and he quickly became a member of the Organizational Council. At that time it was the goal of all young men to achieve precisely what he had managed to do. However, Captain Ehrhardt participated in the capitulation of the government of the November parties, and, like many others, he left the Schwarre Reichswehr. Without a leader he had to face the reality of his country which had fallen prey to chaos.

In 1926, the young Horst at last realized that all those clubs and organizations meant merely the splintering of Germany. He realized that only the rising National Socialist German Labor Party under the leadership of Adolph Hitler offered the possibility of realizing the desired goal. Horst Wessel became a radical socialist.

Having barely become a member of the party, enrolled in the S.A., he was looking for action. Soon enough he found the opportunity for his expansive temperament. At that time there were all kinds of propaganda activities. One important goal was the liberation of Pasewaldli from the Reds. This was particularly important because during the war, Adolph Hitler had been hospitalized there when he was wounded. It was there that he lived during the so called 'German Revolution.' It was there that he first conceived of the possibility of an alternative: a truly national revolution! And so it was fitting that Horst would conquer Pasewalk for the movement.

The young Horst Wessel received his own baptism of fire in that small village. It was there that he earned his spurs. It was there that he was caught up in the rhythm of the songs which he himself sang enthusiastically. 'We are called the Hitler crowds, that is how they know us in the country.' The farmers came to the conclusion that 'those boys are right.' These were the new battles which strengthened the iron resolution of the young fighters not to give in until Germany would be free.

But it was not until Hitler sent Joseph Goebbels to Berlin to deliver his fierce speeches that the true course and leader were shown. Horst Wessel one day delivered a speech and it caught everyone in its spell. Dr. Goebbels noticed him and soon he was, next to the 'Nazi Doctor', the most sought after speaker in the Berlin district. Despite his youth, he succeeded in convincing even old experienced fighters from the other 'camp' (the Reds) to join the National Socialist Movement.

But Horst Wessel was not merely a party member and a speaker. He was above all an S.A. man who contributed his part together with his *mother* to win over parts of the country from control of the Reds and gain them for the Nazi movement... If today the swastika flag is flying over the 'red' northern part of the capital, it is in part due to Horst Wessel.

On the first of May, 1929, he accepted an assignment to lead the 34th troop in the district of Friedrichshain, which enabled him to work in the middle of the 'reddist' part of Berlin. He succeeded in forming the Sturm 5 which was very much feared by the Reds. In masses, the young men came to join him, but he realized that he would only truly deserve the love of his people, who all belonged to the working class, if he would completely share their way of life. So he became a laborer and a work student, and he felt happy among his comrades. However, his actions did not pass unnoticed. It worried the Communists. They had to rap his knuckles! And so the preparations were made for the battle!

Terror

It did not take long until it started. Soon members of the Sturm 5 were attacked in the dark streets of the night. With the increase in the number of incidents, he decided to act. He found the places where the 'criminal mobs' gathered to draw up their murderous plans. Suddenly the telephone cables of a locality were cut, and while some S.A. men watched the streets, Horst Wessel would burst into a Communist local organization, jump on a table and hold a flowing speech. 'If you go on beating up my people, you are in for some surprises.' Then he left, accompanied by some of his own people, and no one dared harm him.

A few days after an unforgettable propaganda tour to Frankfurt, Horst Wessel led his 'Sturm' through 'red' Berlin. Then it was that the still unknown song was heard: *Hoist The Flag* ... The 'red' commune was furious while the other S.A. comrades were enthusiastic and eager to learn the song. Soon everyone knew it and more and more attention was focused on Horst Wessel.

There was a real spirit of comradeship in the Sturm. They stood like one man behind their leader. Despite his youth, he won over all hearts. And one day he held a meeting to collect money ... the money came pouring in. The 'red' Commune was fed up with him, and terror became even more frequent.

Germany, Wake Up

The battle cry of the Hitler movement grew louder through the streets. It became the battle cry of millions. It was hammered into the hearts of the middle class who still remained uncommitted. Horst Wessel was on fire with zeal. He burned with the holy fire for the great cause and he carried the others with him by his songs and his speeches, and by his flaming enthusiasm only known to youth.

It was the great confession nobody had to be ashamed of. He repeated the flaming words written by a German poet, Dietrich Eckart, who, after long years of persecution, found his haven in the mountains of Bayern. He was the first to prophesize about Adolph Hitler. 'That's the man who one day will save Germany.' And he is also buried in the mountains he longed for ...[24]

In this depiction the emphasis is on the martyr as poet, lyricist and composer. Wessel becomes immortal "by the songs ... created for ... people." His love of country is activistic, filled with youthful enthusiasm, and is joined to a natural leadership ability. He is the redeemer of red space, and an inspiration for all who love Germany.

In this next version, the children's version, Wessel's death is dealt with mythically.

Horst Wessel's Last Battle (The Children's Version)

He became tired. Horst Wessel had become tired. It was like at a sword fight, when one contemplates it. Now the adversary is showing an opening, you must get him now. Now. But instead, you do not, or you do it too late, because you are tired. In situations like this the need for self preservation becomes paralyzed, as one finds with tired nations.

In this passage, the message conveyed to the children is that it is dangerous to let down one's guard. One cannot rely on anyone, and if one wants to maintain one's self-preservation, it is best to strike at once. It is dangerous to be tired.

Over and over his comrades insisted – 'Can you trust your landlady? Do you know her well? You had better move because they are after you.' But he did not move out. He wanted events to take their natural course.

She was not to be trusted, the widow Salm. She was an arch-communist and she knew everyone, all the people on Dragonerstrasse. She burst into the pub saying 'He is at home now!' An ugly small Jewess asked 'Who is this 'he'?' 'Now, who else but Wessel? Horst Wessel my nice tenant.'" "It became silent around the tables. A few particularly savage looking fellows suggested that they organize a raid.

But the Jewess scolded 'There is no time to organize, we have to act.' Kuperstein already agreed to the action a long time ago. People in another bar were sent for. There they found Ali, and Kandalskiand, the whole bunch. They formed a council. Since Mrs. Salm had come to tell them that her tenant would not leave, they decided to help her evict him, and in the process nothing could happen to them.

Sixteen people moved to the Frankforterstrasse. Coffee was steaming near the entrance to no. 62. 'You can stand guard at the lookout here, it would not be noticed.' 'Let's go' Cohen was shrieking as if she was afraid that the 'sturm' would wake up their leader. But there

---

[24]Quoted from Die Fahne Hoch, Nazi propaganda booklet. Wiener Library, London, England.

was nobody. The most courageous: Ali, Ruckert and Kandulski, the three Sambrowskis, slipped into the alley. Quickly they released the bolts of their pistols. Mrs. Salm opened the door, and there stood the fellows with their pistols at the ready.

Horst Wessel heard a noise. Who would come to visit him? At that crucial moment, Cohen became afraid. The landlady thought 'what would happen now that she had the murderers together?' Such a chance would not occur again. First softly, and then more strongly, she announced that it was Sturm leader Fiedler. Wessel called 'Come in Richard', and he went to the door and opened it.

There he received a terrible blow – he was shot. He collapsed in the door opening. Some figures moved hurriedly past him towards his writing table.

Mrs. Salm got a paid trip along the Rhine for her trouble. The murderers Ruckert and Hohler were put up at the villa of a regional communist leader. Then Ali drove by car to Prague and Ruckert to Frankfort. The rest of the story you will find out in time.

A paralyzing horror took hold of all the units. They could not believe it, they did not want to believe it in this case. It was as if they had not already heard about thousands of other deaths, and the Red murder wave which is sweeping the country, murders that are continuously more mean and brutal.

It is the cowardice and the betrayal of the enemy which is portrayed here. Despite their 'red' ideology, they take advantage of the luxuries in the society around them. The description is clearly geared toward the arousal of jealousy and further anger.

The men of the S.A. hurried to Wessel's room and placed him on the bed while he was bleeding profusely. But where is the Doctor? The healthy looking man with his kind eyes and serious expression pronounced 'I can't say anything, not yet.' The situation was so serious that Doctor Goebbels was encouraged to come. He immediately postponed a large meeting in the Sportspalast to hurry to the bed of his comrade in arms.

'Doctor?' The Doctor said 'No complications. Perhaps there will be no infection.' Meanwhile the red gangs continued to howl for blood. 'The dog is still alive, that animal will not die.' 'Do you know where he is being kept?' 'In Ward Seven.' 'It's a deal.'

They were laughing. That would be fun tomorrow morning. They would push aside the few nurses at the entrance to the hospital, and force their way into the ward. And this time they would shoot better. Besides, hand grenades would be more sure.

'When?' 'Tomorrow at nine A.M. in the cafe across the street from the hospital.' There were still some decent people, nonetheless, even in groups such as this one, for not all German laborers had been drawn into the net of communism. And so it happened that one of them stole away and ran like a person possessed toward the 'Judenhof.' He wrote a few words on a piece of paper and put it at the entrance of the home of the Wessel family. He then rang the doorbell and ran away.

Wessel's sister immediately informed the S.A. who sounded the alarm. On to Friedrichshain ...!

The corridors were full of 'red.' The only resistance that they put up upon getting their well deserved beating from the S.A. was to shout and bellow. Wessel was saved.

The dying martyr is temporarily spared. His virtues have encouraged defection from the enemy camp. It is the defectors who are decent; the enemy, of course, is treacherous.

'Herr Doctor'

The doctor was satisfied. Until now there had not been any infection. The National Socialists of Berlin and of all Germany were hopeful that Wessel's medical condition would stabilize, but this was not to be the case. Shortly afterwards, the Doctor called for his relatives and for Dr. Goebbels. It was then that he uttered the fateful word 'infection.'

The patient dreamed feverish dreams. About the flag waving high, about his comrades, who, with quiet and steady steps were marching on. About the Fuhrer, whom they greeted, about Goebbels who took care of the enemies of the party, about the police who hounded the Nazis, about dark corners where there was flashing fire, red murder.

'You are not allowed to come near him anymore.' The Sturm were deeply depressed. They strode along past the open door of the sick room with raised arms, and greeted their comrade. Some of them kept watch at the hospital entrance. One could expect anything from those red murderers. Maybe even infection would take too long for their tastes.

German Shame ...

Now Horst Wessel was borne to his grave, and thus started the battle of the coffin. It was horrible, for they had to quarrel with the police about permission to hold the funeral of the beloved deceased. The police would only allow ten cars, no more.

Uniforms. No, these were not allowed. Only those from the Allemannia Wiess Korps and the Normannia Berlin were allowed to appear in uniform. 'The swastika must be removed from the coffin.' 'But Commander...' 'Don't argue with me. My orders are, the flag must be removed, and the other may not be fully hoisted.' It was horrible.

Goering was there, and, of course, Goebbels. Everybody who was of any importance in the National Socialist party in Berlin. They were all present. The population stood behind fences. No one disturbed the procession. The majesty of death was respected.

It was only the fact that the procession had to be accompanied by the rubber sticks of the police that, my young friends, was significant enough to humiliate Germany. A loud noise was heard at the corner of the Weidings and Lothringes Strasse. Among the crowds on the sidewalk one noticed a considerable number of young boys and girls. Suddenly something flew towards the car and hit the hearse. Within a second or two one heard whistling and shouting 'Death to the Nazis.' The next moment one heard the noise of a window breaking. Stones were coming down on those following the car by foot.

The police used force against the mob, who by now had moved very close to the hearse and were tearing at the strings of the wreaths. 'Death to the Nazis.' A few shots were heard and the police were already in the middle of a hand to hand fight.

Then it became quiet again. But the air was threatening. It was obvious by now that the bestiality of those that were bewitched by the Bolsheviks was unlimited. A few streets ahead, in the Koblonlistrasse, a new barrage of stones came down, this time more intensely. Suddenly a cry of anger came from a thousand throats. The police struck blows all around like mad men, but they soon were overpowered. The mob broke through the fence. Two dozen fellows moved towards the hearse. 'Get back' they commanded, and the vehicle was virtually overturned.

The mob also jumped towards the other cars in an attempt to overturn them. Shots were fired and there was a terrible commotion. A particular target for the mob was the car occupied by members of the Corps. A few men jumped on the foot-board of the car and grasped the flag of the Corps. Those in charge drew their swords, blunt parade swords, but the scoundrels became frightened and drew away from the steel. The flag was saved.

When the men of the S.A. arrived, they threw themselves at the Communists with an anger which only the bestiality of the Reds could arouse in a decent German. The Reds were thrown back. Suddenly the rattling tanks were heard. It was indeed a street battle. At a time when a National Socialist hero was buried.

Germany! Germany! in the year of 1930!

At last it quieted down. At last they were nearing the cemetery of St. Nicolai.

It was then that the Germans following the coffin were flushed with embarrassment. On the wall of the cemetery indecent graffiti was chalked. Vile curses defiled the name of Wessel and of our Fuhrer. On the wall of the cemetery!

Germany, not so long ago at all!

Germany of 1930!

At the entrance to the cemetery the Communists suddenly attacked the S.A. men. They were not prepared at all. A raid in a cemetery; no one would expect such a thing in their wildest imagination. Again, violent fighting, again stones and curses. The cemetery was filled with violent action ... The Berlin Korps, and the S.A. climbed the walls and from there struck at the mob.

The mourners had to stand close together. The relatives, Goering, Goebbels. The Fuhrer was ill. He only came later to Horst Wessel. He stood in front of his grave and had a long conversation with one of his most courageous and dedicated men. At that time, at that sad first of March, Hauptmann Von Pfeffer had to speak on behalf of the ill Fuhrer, and lay the wreath.

Then Goering spoke, Goebbels spoke, and the two Rectors of St. Nicolai. Also those in command of the Korps that Horst Wessel belonged to.

There was a great sadness.

Again there were more stones that were thrown at the mourners. The silence which reigned for a moment in the cemetery disappeared with the shouting and the screaming of the mob outside.

But the beloved flag with the swastika was draped over the coffin of Horst Wessel.

Slowly the coffin was lowered.

And then Goering, who seemed deeply upset, neared the grave site and spoke a few more words, and then, overcome with emotion, he threw the helmet of the deceased into the grave.

And then the representative of the Korps stepped forward and threw various hats and bands of Horst Wessel into the grave. Then the flags and standards were lowered. And Wessel's song sounded above his grave: Hoist the Flag, close the ranks. It was an oath, Hoist the Flag, Close the Ranks, the S.A. is marching.

Yes, the S.A. would march against millions of enemies, towards the self determination and the reawakening of Germany. Towards honor. And never again would a German have to be buried amidst the curse of animal Reds.

I would not say that it was the sacred oath at the grave site of Horst Wessel, this funeral, (which more than anything else, demonstrated the degree of German distress and humiliation), which did indeed awaken the German nation within three years. For it was in precisely the same year, the year of the death of Horst Wessel, that the National Socialist party captured 107 seats in the Reichstag.

Did the murderer Ali even conceive of this as a possibility? After he committed the murder, they sent him by car. Not to reward him, but merely to avoid exposing the party. However, when Ali wanted to continue his pleasant way of living in Prague, he was told that they could do very well without him. He had done his job already.

Sulking Ali returned to Berlin. There he was taken prisoner at last, together with his accomplices. At that time, the punishment for murder was mild. Hohler and Ruckert got away with six years in the house of corrections. Randulski got five years ... Sombrowski two years, Willi and Walter Sambrowski one and a half years. Honeclick one year. The two women involved, Cohen and Salm, got only one year, and Kuferstein, the Moscow intelligence officer, got only four months.

The Meaning of the Horst Wessel Legend

I say legend because the figure of Horst Wessel will enter the German legends like other heroes of the history of Germany. Body and mind, mind and body, only when those two are united can they realize an idea, push a nation forward.

The idea alone is useless. If there are no fists available to force a way for that idea.

The Marxist preached with the dogma of fists and violence, with the terror of the proletariats, and used the raised fist as the German greeting. Against this terror an idea is not very effective. There should be, instead, young heroes who answer terror by terror.

Fist, body, mind, and idea determine the movement. It constitutes a sacrifice to rob, fight, and maybe be killed for an idea. It is Sacrifice, but it is also idealism, my dear young friends.

And Horst Wessel is not that sacred song of that idealism. Without idealism there is no war. Without idealism there is no edification. Without idealism and the readiness to sacrifice there is no national community and no socialism of the people. Without idealism the word of the Fuhrer's would not exist. *You are nothing. The Nation is everything.*

Without idealism, there is no beauty in life, no culture. Idealists have built up the Greek-Northern culture, idealists have spread Christianity. Idealists have freed Germany from Napoleon. Idealists twice entered the heart of France. Idealists have built for the third time a German Empire.

If you go now, my young friends, to your elders, those who have standing in practical life, with their concern about money and their own personal advancement, their purely practical orientation might strike you as not being very decent.

Their concerns, however, are explicable, but only to a certain extent. In all fairness, their lives are the product of events of the past. However, young people who are not idealists, are despicable.

Therefore, the ideal of the young German is the S.A. man. Therefore, Horst Wessel is the ideal of the young S.A. man.[25]

In addition to this rather simple minded version for children, there were many other attempts to 'explain' the meaning of the Horst Wessel martyrdom. They were, for the most part, based on interpretations of Goebbels. On the day of Wessel's death, in an ecstatic vision of future Nazism, Goebbels exclaimed that "Horst Wessel will be among the workers and students when they march together into the future in a German Germany, when they will sing his song, all together. For today, throughout the country, the brown soldiers are now singing the song. Within ten years, children at school, workers in the factories, and

---

[25]From Erich Czech Joschberg, *Das Jugendbuch Von Horst Wessel* (1933).

soldiers on the roads will be singing it. His song makes him immortal. I see groups too numerous to count, marching along forever. A mortified, fallen people has risen and is in motion. The awakening Germany is demanding its rights: Freedom and Bread! The banners are waving, the drums are booming, the flutes are jubilant. And from the throats of the millions comes the song of the German revolution. Hoist the Flag." (Dr. Goebbels, Feb. 23, 1930. The day of Horst Wessel's death.)

The most explicit recognition of Horst Wessel's important place in the Nazi pantheon of Saints and martyrs is to be found in a Nazi publication by Wilfred Bade.[26] In this publication one finds explicit recognition for the importance of martyrdom and its alleged impact. It is a veritable sociological theory of martyrdom, and it emphasizes a number of significant points.

1. The first point stressed is that a martyr emerges after his death. Neither the supporter of the martyr, nor his enemies are certain that, in truth, they understand the historical meaning of the death. Its meaning is only revealed retrospectively. By stressing this point of view, it is clear that a conspiratorial view of events is prevented. The martyr emerges in a mysterious way which is not amenable to rational planning and certainly is incapable of being fabricated.

2. Although the full meaning is only revealed retrospectively, the publication then stresses that there are, nonetheless, those that can foresee the future. It is this prescience of supporters which lends greater dignity to their leadership, while the prescience of enemies lends greater nefariousness to their schemings. The prescience of spectators (like the farmers) lends credence to the correctness of their ultimate judgement.

3. To strengthen the martyr myth, the counter- productive efforts made by the martyr's enemies are in inverse proportion to their secret recognition and forebodings that he is indeed a most potent martyr.

4. The effectiveness of martyrdom as an irrevocable symbol is given implicit recognition in the publication.

5. Whereas in most cases death is seen as the conclusion of life, martyrdom brings about a transformation in perspective. "Life meant only the preparation for the death that was intended by fate." The theory of this transformation is presented.

6. This transformation of perspective is associated with the overpowering influence of 'fate', and fate is associated with the change of 'eras', and with the symbolically powerful discovery of a great victim.

---

[26]W. Bade, *The Theory of Martyrological Efficacy*, pp. 20-41.

7. When all of the above takes place, one can expect miracles – a miracle which even the enemies of the movement must acknowledge.

This is the theory of martyrological efficacy stated in its most blatant form. The question is, Are the claims made for martyrological theory true? The following portion of the Bade book demonstrates all the points laid down in the theory:

> Horst Wessel died on Feb. 13, 1930, twenty two and a half years old. He was buried in the midst of stone throwing, and an outrage of uncontrolled hatred. This could only be explained at a later stage, when the task which fate bestowed upon Horst Wessel became clear. Although at the time of his death the S.A. and the National Socialists already understood his call, the great masses of people would only understand later on. There were, however, some who must have understood something at the time of his burial. To judge from the vehemence of the Berlin Communists, they too must have had a clear idea about it as well. They must have realized that they were losing the battle over Germany, just when they believed that by shooting down Horst Wessel, they had won the battle. They therefore tried to destroy everything that was left of him. Anything that could possibly symbolize him would pose a threat to his murderers.

> During the funeral procession, tens of thousands of people stood in the streets who, until then, had only heard about Horst Wessel as an active member of the National Socialist movement in Berlin. They had heard that he was the leader of the Fifth Sturm of the Berlin S.A. and that he wrote the song 'Hoist the Flag, The Ranks Firmly Closed.'

> Germany realized that something of utmost importance had happened, something irrevocable, which could lead only to eternal downfall or to eternal victory.

> Because a victim had fallen.

> Before his death, his life was not of great importance or very meaningful. Whereas for millions of people, death means the end of life, in the case of Horst Wessel, life meant only the preparation for the death that was intended by fate.

> Such a turnabout in the values of life and death of human beings is always a sign of the true-victim, the one that is destined by fate. It is at the moment of the sacrifice that it becomes clear that the course of events are dictated by fate. The sorrow and pain are overshadowed by the pride that results from the insight that just this man was chosen for this highest mission.

> There are only a few great victims in world history. But when they occur, it means that an era has ended, sometimes an era of thousands of years, and that a new form has developed for thousands of years to come.

> *People call such a sacrificial death martyrdom, and its effects they rightly call miracles.*

> Such a miracle happened in 1930 to the National Socialist movement. And since the realization of a miracle is an undeniable

fact, the murderers also realized that they had acted under the compulsion of fate to bring into being a process which they had intended to avoid at all costs. But to no avail.

An overlooked aspect of the social mobilization literature is that in order to mobilize people, it is necessary to tell them a narrative around which they can mobilize.[27] As we shall now see, included in the adult version of the Horst Wessel myth were all the major elements necessary to mobilize a population.

1. Every effort is made to stress the respectability of Wessel's background. He was the oldest son of the Minister D. Ludwig Wessel and Margarette, also the daughter of a Minister. At the outbreak of World War I, Horst's father was the first to volunteer as an army chaplain, and he served in Belgium, Russia and the Balkans. The message is clear that Horst Wessel is from a family dedicated to Germany.

2. Sprinkled in the narrative are a number of authenticating details. For example, the Wessel family lived in Berlin in the Judenstrasse near the Judenhof. The added detail is supplied that the Wessel home was located in the very center of the Berlin Jewish ghetto, and an old acacia tree, purported to be the symbolic tree of the Jews, was growing there.

3. Inconsolability after the tragedy of the Versailles Treaty, and the search for the 'true Germany', are two themes that are stressed. Within Germany there was a frantic search for the true essence of the German people. It was the anxiety surrounding a lost but desired object, and this was the anxiety which supposedly moved Horst Wessel. Both the search and the inconsolability blended with a fear of threatened total annihilation.

In the Horst Wessel narrative, all these themes are associated with the death of Horst's father. "Horst Wessel grew up quickly. At the time of the Treaty of Versailles, he understood very well the implications of that horrible piece of paper, but he saw no way which could lead to freedom. His father had returned from war but could not console him. Then his father died. His relatives could not help him in his search for Germany. He knew that he had to fight so that Germany would not be removed from the congregation of nations, so that two thousand years of German history would not disappear into nameless shame."

The joy of the father's return, the inability of the father to explain the 'peace', the death of the father, the inconsolability of the son over the lost Germany, the fear of a total annihilation of Germany's

---

[27]c.f. Etzioni, *The Active Society* (1968), especially pp. 443-445; 535-537.

historical significance – all these combined in one particular description of public anxiety of which Wessel was the symbol. "Many people thought like Horst Wessel; there was a general resoluteness abroad that people should get organized and disciplined in order to face the enemy and fight with the same means that the enemy had used in order to gain power."

4. The solution to the general disconsolation is not to be found in prayer or in intellectual activity. "Very disappointed, Horst Wessel buried himself in his books. He finished school and entered the University, but the lectures about Roman law did not engage him." It was not from the realm of ideas that the solution would come, but from political activity. "And there, (in politics) he found the ideas he had been searching for during the previous years, which would give him a necessary strength to create the New Germany."

The solution is not in the leftist class struggle, but rather in disciplined organization. Wessel sought a movement with the necessary discipline and professionalism. He tried first the Reichswehr, then the Bismark Bund, then the Nilung of Captain Erhardt, and finally the National Socialist movement.

5. Political activity is a central theme in the narrative. It's goal was to defuse the proletarian class struggle by creating a community of workers which included members of the middle class. By removing the threat of middle class persecution, "there was no need for revolution from below, for such a struggle had lost its suicidal justification."

6. There is a disdain for the use of verbal methods – talk, argument, discussion, ideas. It is through fists that the real Germany will be recovered, that things will be settled. Fists are the tools of the opposition and any other methods are impotent. One senses a radical impatience with the slow methods of persuasion.

7. Truly committed members of the National Socialist movement have no concern for either their personal safety or their health. "He even impressed the Communists, who let him know that they would regret it if they were forced to use other than verbal arguments to stop his activities. Horst Wessel did not mention these threats to his comrades, but instead continued his work with even greater zeal." He refuses to take the advice of his mother and to remove himself from danger. Even his family's seductive offer of a trip to South America is refused, and an assignment by the Movement to a less exposed position is rejected.

8. In the narrative, Wessel has become the true embodiment of the cause. He was capable of speaking in the name of the cause through a mystic union too mysterious and wonderful to fathom. "He became the example, the symbol, the realization of the National Socialist man, as

the Fuhrer envisaged in the future. He was not aware of it himself, but others were. They began to watch him. His songs, which he wrote for his Sturm, were sung by the S.A. within weeks. Through his mouth the movement itself was speaking."

It is this capacity to bespeak the "thoughts, battles, suffering, beliefs and victories" of the movement that lends special poignancy to the fact that Wessel was wounded in the mouth. The message communicated is that the enemies are trying to destroy his capacity to speak.

9. So dreadful is the deed perpetuated on Wessel by his enemies, that it is unthinkable that it could have been done without serious reservations and moral reluctance. Suspense and drama must be added to the story through the introduction of an arch-enemy. Most enemies, despicable as they are, have a conscience, but the arch-enemy does not. "Twice even those heartless creatures hesitated. Twice the Jewess pushed them forward. Then at last it happened. There was a knock on Horst Wessel's door."

10. The temporary improvement in Horst Wessel's condition is a suspenseful remission right out of Greek drama. The temporary remission of a dying martyr has some uses. While he is lingering, there is time to prove that there are those among the enemy who will betray their evil plans, to make the enemy less secure in their bonds of loyalty. Unless you are a member of the Nazi movement, you can never be sure that someone in your movement will not betray you. True comradery is only possible in the Nazi movement.

The more nefarious the plan against the Nazi movement, the more apt one is to find someone willing to betray the plan. "For one month the National Socialist Movement feared for Horst Wessel's life. One instant it seemed as if death would pass him by. The fever went down, the wounded hero was able to receive his district leader and his friends. Then the Commune decided upon an attack on the hospital. But someone from the K.P.D. had a bout of conscience. An anonymous letter informed his sister of the intended attack, and when the Communists arrived, members of the Sturm stood in the corridors of the ward where the fatally wounded Horst Wessel was lying, and succeeded in pushing the Communists back in a bitter fight lasting fifteen minutes. From that day on the room of Horst Wessel was guarded continuously by the S.A. But this demonstration of comradery could not save him from death. On the 23rd of February, 1930, Horst Wessel died. A sacrifice had been made. From his spilled blood the Third Reich rises, dedicated to eternity ..."[28]

---

[28]W. Bade, *The Theory of Martyrological Efficacy*, p. 20-41.

The Nurse's Version

The nurse's version of the Horst Wessel myth is deserving of analysis before we turn to information from behind the scenes which was not used in the Nazi propaganda. We will analyze the relevant points after the narrative is presented.

> This is the account of a nurse who works at the Hospital in the working class district of northern Berlin, in the red building of the former Am Friedrishshain. The hospital is now called the Horst Wessel hospital. It was in Building Number 7, a two storey building, that Horst Wessel died. While in the garden of that hospital I met a nurse, Helene Richlin, who nursed Horst Wessel for five weeks prior to his death. She told me the following:

> 'Our hospital, which by rights should be a refuge for all sick and suffering, became a treatment center for countless victims of political confrontations between 1929-1930. The victims were both Communists and National Socialists. I myself did not understand a thing about politics at that time. When I arrived at work on the morning of January 15, 1930, I was told by the night sister that she had received a serious case during the night.'

The hospital where Wessel died was later named after him. Although it is not noted in the nurse's narrative, there is a contradiction between the nurse's vision of a hospital as a refuge for sick and suffering, and the naming of that hospital after the dedicated victim of a specific cause.

The nurse here qualifies as a credible witness to Wessel's heroic death in her disclaimer that she did not understand a thing about politics. However, she is quick to add "at that time" lest the reader think that anyone could possibly not understand the sacred nature of politics after the advent of the Nazi regime.

He Only Talked About His Ideas

> I stood near the bed where the patient was lying. He could not talk because his tongue was swollen. On the sign above his bed was written – Horst Wessel, 22 years old. His temperature was very low, probably due to excessive bleeding.

> He became one of my many patients. It was not merely his serious condition which made an impression on me, it was mainly his courageous behavior and the whole personality of this severely wounded young man which continually impressed me.

> During the first hours, before he was able to speak, he wrote his wishes down on a piece of paper. Soon after, he began to talk. He hardly ever complained about his pain, he only talked about his ideas. He remembered exactly all the details of the murderous attack on him. He said 'I always expected something like this to happen one day. My landlady certainly associated with them. Everything happened so quickly. I was not at all prepared. I was sitting at my desk

and working when suddenly I heard someone asking outside my door, 'Is Horst Wessel there?'

'I thought it was a friend. I opened the door and immediately the shooting started before anything could be said. I heard the explosion, felt the blood run warm over my neck. Everything happened so quickly. They did not say anything but then left immediately. I must have lost consciousness.'

It was while telling about those events that Horst Wessel became very animated. However, when he talked about his goals his brown eyes sparkled. He was the happiest when his friends came to visit him. They came every day. 'I can rely on my boys', he often declared proudly.

Wessel demonstrates our theme of the martyr who manages to transcend his own embodiment. We are told that he is only concerned with ideas. In another version, the doctor reports that the bullet was lodged in Wessel's vertebrae, but here we are told that he could barely talk and his tongue was swollen. In spite of his pain and his extensive bleeding, he 'only talked of his ideas.'

After authenticating the sequence of events which the Nazi party had announced, Wessel reasserts his trust and confidence in his fellow Nazis. He declares proudly that he can rely on "his boys."

On one occasion when his friends came to visit, as they were standing in the doorway, they called out, 'Now you try to be all right Horst', whereupon he turned to me and said 'Doesn't that make one happy, nurse? That alone makes getting oneself shot worthwhile.' His sufferings must have brought him great happiness, for he realized just how much love and loyalty his friends had for him.

Once I said to him 'Horst Wessel, I can understand you so well because my favorite poet is Fritz Reuter who spent seven years in prison for his ideas.' 'But nurse Helene! Fritz Reuter and us? That is no fair comparison! We are making history!!'

In these paragraphs two central themes are highlighted. Wessel found his suffering easy because of his strong bonds of communion with his comrades. His sufferings even brought him happiness because his friends displayed such fierce loyalty to him.

In addition, he was quick to disclaim any similarity between himself and a mere poet like Fritz Reuter. Wessel's suffering was 'making history.'

In spite of the enthusiasm that he demonstrated when discussing his ideas, he was obviously severely injured. He, nonetheless, never complained. Sometimes he noted that his throat hurt where the lethal injury was located. He was particularly animated and lively the last few days before his death.

On Monday Dr. Goebbels was to visit him. Horst Wessel was in good spirits and pleaded with me 'Today my friend is coming, please let him stay longer than usual.' 'Yes, only if you promise not to talk, only listen.' 'I promise, and furthermore, whatever Dr. Goebbels is going to tell could not possibly be harmful for me.' At half past two Dr. Goebbels did come and I told him that the patient should talk as little as possible.

Every time I entered the room Horst Wessel begged me to allow his friend to stay for another ten minutes. When at last the Doctor left, he said to me 'I have to travel to Munich, will I ever see him alive again?' I evaded giving a direct answer. When I returned, I found Horst Wessel's face radiant. 'You don't know fully why this is such a beautiful day for me. It is going well.'

'What is going so well?' I asked. 'Our movement.' That day he ate well for the first time, and assured me that food have never tasted so well. He was sure he was going to recover.

Goebbels, the master propogandist of Nazi Germany, is sardonically portrayed as a friend who could never have anything harmful to say. Goebbels, of course, is instructed to do most of the talking. He brings the glad tidings that the movement is doing well, and thus the patient is radiant and can eat well for the first time. His body and soul are totally bound with the welfare of the movement.

The Last Hours

For a few days the situation remained unchanged, but on Friday, he took a turn for the worse. Saturday he was in agony. The doctors did what they could. His mother and sister were there and his friend Sturmfuhrer Fiedler. He asked me whether he would be allowed to bring in some friends.

When we returned with fifteen of Wessel's most loyal friends, he was lying with his eyes closed and breathing with difficulty. When he noticed the presence of his comrades, with his last bit of strength he lifted his right arm to greet them.

At the foot of his bed his mother and sister were seated. I was standing near the head of the bed. Sometimes his mouth formed words but we could not understand him. Outside the door his friends kept guard. I remained at his side until one o'clock in the morning.

The next day, Horst Wessel died.

Following the temporary remission, the agony starts. Wessel cannot speak when his friends enter, but he is strong enough to greet them with the upraised right arm. It is not the last words of Horst Wessel which is the lasting image, but the gesture of comradery and loyalty to his friends.

The Factual Story of Horst Wessel

In 1935, Alfred Apfel, a distinguished attorney of Weimar Germany who defended many dissidents and political nonconformists, published a book about German justice from behind the scenes. It is from this book that the factual story of Horst Wessel emerges. Apfel records his astonishment when he discovers that the hero of the National Socialist Anthem is none other than Horst Wessel, a former client of his.

> In an uninterrupted stream, huge hordes of Brownshirts marched in procession down the Kurfurstendamm, where I lived, with cries of 'Heil' and songs of their party. Among these songs, the tunes of which were mostly stolen from the Communists, one in particular struck my ear, because it was most often repeated. Later I was to hear it not hundreds, but thousands of times more. It was made the national anthem, and it resounds on every possible and impossible occasion, at official parades, at opening nights of plays, at school celebrations and at funerals.
>
> Not until some weeks later did I learn that this hymn was called the Horst Wessel song. The name Horst Wessel sounded somewhat familiar, I seemed to have heard it somewhere, though I could not immediately place it. Suddenly I remembered. In one of the numerous trials I had conducted during the past years, I had as a client the alleged murderer of a certain Horst Wessel. My client's profession had been that of a pimp, and recollecting the circumstances of that case, I dismissed it as incredible that this Horst Wessel could be one and the same as the new national hero of the German people. Why I was unable to believe this, and why, even today, I still think I am dreaming when I hear of the man who is being held up to the youth of Germany as their new ideal, the reader will comprehend when he hears the story of my experience.[29]

Apfel was brought into the defense of Ali Hohler, who had been charged with the murder of Horst Wessel, by Hohler's girlfriend. From visits to Hohler in prison, the following facts emerged: Hohler was a known criminal with a long series of arrests and detentions in various prisons. He belonged to a well known, well organized criminal gang called the Ring Society, which was reputed to include the most incorrigible criminals in German society. The Society was known for its brutality, but also for its code of conduct which included social welfare provisions for the families of incarcerated members, and an elaborate set of comic-tragic rituals for funeral internment.

On the day in question, Hohler told Apfel that he was celebrating with friends of the Society a particularly successful haul he had made. The celebration, which took place in a beerhall, was interrupted when

---

[29]Apfel, A. *Behind the Scenes of German Justice* (1939), pp. 156-157.

a group of men, accompanied by an old woman, came into the beerhall. The woman claimed that she had a roomer who refused to pay her the rent due her. Since the landlady's husband had been a friend of the Society members, she had been told that she could get help from them if she ever got into a fix. Under Apfel's prodding questions, Hohler indicated that his sole motivation had been the desire to help a friend. There had been no political motive at all. In fact, Hohler was quite indignant at the suggestion that he might have done what he subsequently did for political motives. Politics meant nothing at all in his circle. Their sole interest was personal gain.

Hohler became particularly indignant when he heard that the roomer who refused to pay was Horst Wessel. He regarded Wessel as a rival pimp because Wessel had a girl working the streets for him in a district that Hohler considered his own province. He decided to join the group who were going to teach Wessel a lesson.

When they got to the woman's apartment, Hohler approached the door. "I knocked at the door – no answer. I knock again. After a while, the door opens just a crack, very slowly, and I see him. Instead of asking what I want, he puts his hand into his back pocket so quick that I can see what he's after. Rather than let him do the shooting, I pull out my own gun instead, and let him have four or five shots in the middle of his mug. In two ticks I am downstairs again, and back at the party."[30] Hohler then went into hiding, but was ultimately apprehended and brought to trial. The trial attracted enormous attention, and Hohler was joined in the docket by all who had conspired with him in the act.

To the dismay of the Nazis, it emerged at the trial that Wessel had become disenchanted with the Nazi party. He was withdrawn and morose, and was totally resigned to living a parasitic life from the earnings of his girlfriend who plied her trade in the streets of Berlin. However, by the time the trial began, the Goebbels Nazi propaganda machine was too committed to the Wessel legend to renounce Wessel without serious harm to the movement. Goebbels decided to brazen it out.

Apfel notes that "For a long time (after the trial), the Hitler party preserved a very well-advised silence with respect to Horst Wessel. It takes all the unlimited and cynical insolence of Dr. Goebbels, the Minister of Propaganda, to fill the need for a national hero by picking out a Horst Wessel for glorification. Dr. Goebbels knows perfectly well who and what Horst Wessel was, having been present often with his staff while the trial was in progress."[31]

---

[30]Ibid, p. 161.
[31]Ibid, p. 165.

It was precisely this "unlimited and cynical insolence" that made the glorification of Wessel so attractive to Goebbels. Reiss' biography of Goebbels records the special thrill he got out of presenting the inherently perverse as the genuine article. Anyone could create a martyr out of a spotless, sincere sacrifice for the Nazi cause. But only a genius of propaganda could take a disenchanted pimp through a program of glorification and turn him into a national youth hero.

Although the popularity of his song and the following he had did contribute to the success of the Wessel myth, nonetheless, it was the feat of brazening it out which demonstrated that the people's desire to believe was stronger than the facts. The importance of Goebbels's work was shown by the inability of the facts to compromise the Wessel legend. It did not matter that Wessel was publicly compromised, that he failed to get proper treatment because his comrades refused to have him treated by an available Jewish doctor. What was important was that it was possible to perpetuate the fiction of Wessel's total devotion to the Nazi cause, of his uncompromising commitment to his party's work, his neglect of his own pleasures and satisfactions, and the loyalty of his comrades no matter what the circumstances.

With exasperation and irony Apfel writes: "It only remains to note that good days indeed have come to the guild of pimps, when one of their number has been raised to the glory of declared national hero of the New Germany."[32]

Horst Wessel and the Fabrication of Conviction

On February 23, 1930, Goebbels's ten year search for the perfect Nazi martyr came to an end. On this day, Horst Wessel, the twenty two year old sometime pimp was elevated to the top of the Nazi pantheon of dead saintly heroes. Henceforth, at the start of each mass meeting, Hitler's loyal followers chanted in unison a response to the question "Horst Wessel, Bist du ihr?" (Horst Wessel, are you here?). Hundreds, thousands, tens of thousands, hundreds of thousands, and even millions would shout in response, "Ya, Ich bin yest" (yes, I am here).

There can be no rationally justified reasons for queries to the dead. However, Nazi predilections for astrology and necromancy aside, there were some very good reasons why the dead Horst Wessel should be asked if he was still there. These reasons relate to the need of group leaders to create for their followers some deeply held beliefs that both satisfy their followers' needs, and coincidentally strengthen the interests of the wielders of power.

---

[32]Ibid, p. 166.

All groups ultimately rest not only on power and coercion, but on the consent of the governed, however tenuously granted. No instruments of violence can successfully manage to subdue the multitude, unless there is a modicum of consent to their reign. In addition, leaders desire and require more than a reluctantly granted consent to their hegemony. They want enthusiasm and support. It is not public opinion that leaders want on their side, but a deeper reassurance that their supporters acquiesce to their leadership and projects. Conviction is a quality that wielders of power seek in their followers.

However, true conviction requires a willingness to die for the cause. This is the significance of the martyr in history. The martyr is the quintessential example of conviction. It would appear that no culture, no group, no grand idea can do without a martyr to make it plausible. It is conviction here which is the key. Not opinion, belief or attitude which can be effervescent, but dedicated conviction. Any assault on conviction is, in effect, an assault on the social bond, on the possibilities of being human. To be human, one must have the possibility of conviction.

And what is conviction? "Convictions are the beliefs which make people what they are."[33] "We are," said Zuurberg, "our convictions."[34] A human being never comes as a carte blanche to consider a set of beliefs. In addition to the positive persistence of an obstinately held belief or opinion, individuals are also transformed by *not* holding to a belief. Conviction, thus, carries with it the implication not only of a fixed belief, but also of having been persuaded by argument or proof. It implies a conversation, an argument, a challenge, and having been conquered by an alternative set of beliefs.

By overcoming previously held beliefs, leaders hope to arouse in their adherents not only the positive predisposition to their legitimacy as leaders, but the deeply held and stubborn conviction which can successfully mobilize these adherents into positive action. It was precisely the creation of such a community of conviction which the fabricators of the Horst Wessel legend had in mind. Unfortunately, in their very success, they have demonstrated that conviction is value neutral. It adheres to good causes as well as to bad, and the success of types like Goebbels constitutes the greatest challenge to conviction in our times.

For the past forty years or so, the major weight of opinion in intellectual circles is that we are all more likely to be destroyed by those who have convictions than to be saved. Albert Camus made the

---

[33]McClendon & Smith, *Understanding Religious Convictions* (1975), p. 8.
[34]Ibid, p. 58.

original statement to this effect after World War II.[35] The theme was taken up in the movement of intellectuals away from matters of conviction, towards a kind of "conviction against conviction," with a program of radical doubt about the salutary effects of any kind of conviction in the world, except, of course, its own. Thus Goebbels and the powerful Horst Wessel myth has had a boomerang impact on the post World War II world of conviction, and martyrdom is viewed with fear and skepticism among the intellectuals of the west.

---

[35]Camus, A., *Neither Victims nor Executioners.*

Part Three

CONVICTION:
THE MODERN DILEMMA

6

Modern Man, Conviction and Martyrdom

Unlike the classical examples of martyrological conviction which we have discussed, contemporary western man has been characterized as preoccupied with the self.[1] Indeed, as community structure and family bonds weaken, it is the self which is regarded as the new center, which holds together as all ties weaken. This point of view has been recognized since Durkheim's writing on the cult of the person.[2]

In the past, the communal ties of culture and religion were the key determinants of limits and permissions. The individual knew what could and could not be done through the dictates of the society in which he or she lived. This is no longer true for modern man. Culture has loosened its capacity to influence the choices of the individual, and the burden of choice now falls on the self.

In an interesting and engaging book[3], Phillip Reiff has indicated that for the individual who is bereft of communal ties and who must meet the world without their protective armor, psychological treatment becomes an accepted need. "When so little can be taken for granted, and when the meaningfulness of social existence no longer grants an inner life at peace with itself, every man must become something of a genius about himself."[4] The individual then develops an "analytic attitude" toward himself based on the insights of various contemporary therapies. Building on Reiff's work, it is the content of that analytic attitude and its relation to conviction which we will now discuss.

---

[1]Lasch, C. *The Culture of Narcissism* (1979).
[2]E. Durkheim: The Cult of the Self.
[3]Reiff, P. *The Triumph of the Therapeutic*.
[4]Ibid, p. 15.

For contemporary man with an analytic attitude, an important prerequisite is to develop a mindset which tries to keep options open at all times, and thereby avoid commitments. According to this point of view, there are no absolute or intrinsic hierarchies of goals and values, and it is important to maintain multiple perspectives. Psychological clarity about oneself supersedes commitment to any societal value.

This ideal of 'hanging loose' and seeing the self and its dictates as the center is echoed in some of the popular forms of therapy. It is summarized in Fritz Perls' Gestalt Therapy Prayer:

I do my thing and you do your thing

I am not in this world to live up to your expectations

And you are not in this world to live up to mine.

You are you and I am I;

If by chance we find each other, it's beautiful

If not, it can't be helped.

What this 'prayer' connotes is a firm denial that we are here to live up to each others' expectations. Unlike the martyrs who sacrifice their lives for the group and its convictions, we are not here to live up to traditions handed down to us through culture or religion. Quite the contrary, the only worthwhile struggle is to free ourselves of each others' grasp, in order to turn around and "by chance" find each other again. According to the analytic attitude, for modern man the highest good is an affirmation of "my thing," and the ability to reject what is asked and found unsuitable. With this solipsistic faith in the centrality of the self, there can be no certainty that meaningful connections can be made with others.

Although there are modern therapies and credos which have different perspectives, the analytic attitude and the Gestalt principles which have been presented are pervasive in American culture and are important guidelines for many millions in the western world.[5] As we have suggested, it is difficult to imagine a mindset which is further from that of the martyr and the deep commitment to conviction which the martyr as a social type represents.

In a hypothetical meeting between a martyr and a psychologically oriented individual with an analytic attitude, one finds a meeting between two individuals with very different commitments. Most immediately blatant is the contrast between a commitment to knowing and feeling one's inner essence, and a commitment to the fulfillment of a moral purpose. The dispute between them would be over self or cause as

---

[5]c.f. the documentation of this thesis in Bellah, et. al., *Habits of the Heart, Individualism and Commitment in American Life* (1985). Especially Chapter 5.

the central object of conviction. To the psychological man, "clarity about oneself supercedes devotion to an ideal as the model of right conduct."[6] From his perspective, the martyr appears to be fanatically escaping from the self examination which should be his major preoccupation.

In the therapeutic mind set it is the process of choice which becomes more significant than the object of that choice. Since this process is of such significance to the psychological man, a proper emotional distance must be achieved. There is a danger when one object of choice is taken too seriously, because all the other available options will not be given a fair chance. The martyr appears in his eyes as a fanatic with unresolved psychological problems which have forced him to close his options. The martyr's conviction represents a premature closure. Perhaps a better cause will come along tomorrow. Perhaps the cause will be discredited or demonstrated to be a psychological aberration, a fraud or a dangerous illusion. Besides, why be so morbid and give up the good things in life?

For the martyr, of course, the cause is the central issue, not the options available or the process of identifying with that cause. The martyr would see the psychological man as hopelessly fragmented and in search of guidance from a fickle self. He is unstable and set on a quest which is doomed to failure. When nothing is held dear, and all options are open, there are no absolute values with which to give meaning to the world. Although maintaining open options appears to represent such a choice, it is a choice which lacks moral vigor. The good that such a position affirms has no specific content, and has no staying power against evil other than the commitment to free options. In addition, a concentration exclusively on the self as life's quintessential project precludes all other commitments, because the layers of the self do not lead into the world, but just ever deeper into the self.

Although the martyr is generally depicted as other-worldly, from this interchange it appears that this is not the case. The martyr's path must lead through this world even though its destination is posthumous existence. It is the psychological man who, in the end, is more world denying. In reality, the self is as much an abstraction and a mystic entity as the world to come. No one has ever seen or touched the self, and it is a social convention which barely existed for much of recorded history. The irony is that the project of psychological man, although

---

[6]"Triumph of the Therapeutic," p. 56. Bellah has stated the case even more radically than Rieff. According to Bellah et. al., "The therapeutic view not only refuses to take a moral stand, it actively distrusts 'morality' ..." p. 129, *Habits of the Heart*.

self affirming, is ultimately world denying, while the martyr, who is self denying is ultimately world affirming.

The martyr is not a pluralist, nor a relativist, particularly when it comes to his own convictions. It is not objective detachment which the martyr seeks but passionate commitment. To be possessed by some great and transcendent purpose. The psychological man, on the other hand, seeks to survive and is skeptical about the worth of ultimate commitments. These are two very different world views, and life perspectives.

Modern Man, Convictions and Martyrdom

It seems to be particularly difficult to believe in causes nowadays. The psychological climate discourages commitment and the media present us with a constant debunking, so that frequently, yesterday's cause is today's fraud. Widespread skepticism is not only a response to the media, but to both the history of the 20th century, with its mass murders and final solutions, and to an awareness that the stakes are too high for an apocalyptic showdown between antagonistic convictions. Nothing seems worth such a risk.

And yet, without convictions we cannot live a life of meaning. Without a dedication to values neither culture nor religion is plausible, and our doubts about the purpose of life go unanswered. Without our convictions, we are less than human.

On the Passion for Martyrdom in a Therapeutic Age

During the era of self-involvement, why should martyrdom be a subject of attention? According to Bellah (Bellah et.al. 1985), the therapeutic ideology is central to the value system of America. Building on the insights of Durkheim and Reiff, Bellah argues that the therapeutic ideology "proffers a normative order of life, with character ideals, images of the good life, and methods of attaining it. Yet it is an understanding of life generally hostile to older ideas of moral order. Its center is the autonomous individual, presumed able to choose the roles he will play and the commitments he will make, not on the basis of higher truths but according to the criterion of life effectiveness as the individual judges it ... it enables the individual to think of commitments – from marriage and work to political and religious involvements – as enhancements of the sense of individual well being rather than as moral imperatives."[7]

Commitments such as personal obligation, moral responsibility and self sacrifice are deemed inappropriate for decision making. In fact, "the therapeutic view not only refuses to take a moral stand, it

---

[7]Bellah, p. 47.

actively distrusts "morality..."[8] The governing principles are, instead, psychic gratification, personal fulfillment, open honest communication and an emphasis on individualism.

Assuming that Bellah is correct in his analysis, one would expect martyrdom to play a very small role in modern therapeutic consciousness. Martyrs can hardly be said to possess the characteristics of the well analyzed analysand and they are anything but role models for the therapeutic age.

However, quite the contrary is true. Martyrs appear to be very much with us in the last decades of the twentieth century. Although we have not made a systematic content analysis of newspapers and weekly news magazines, we have noticed over the years that hardly a week goes by without stories about martyrs in the mass media. The list is a long one.

Only a few years ago, the interest in the Jonestown mass suicide became a veritable cottage industry. The martyrs of Solidarity, the Polish workers' uprising, have been fully covered in the media. Two popular and recently elected heads of state, Corazon Aquino and Benazir Bhutto, owe their offices to the political martyrdom of members of their families. A prominent member of the Sandinista regime in Nicaragua owes her right to political dissent and perhaps her life to the martyrizing of her husband who was killed in the Sandinista cause. The Palestine Liberation Organization is continuously claiming martyr status for those killed in the struggle for the Palestinian state, and the world continues its fascination with the martyr warriors of Shiite Iran and the self flagellating religious culture which encourages them.

The period following the second world war has been consistently concerned with martyrdom. To this day articles appear in many periodicals about Rosa Luxemborg, the martyr of communism. The Catholic church and the world media made a grand celebration out of the declaration of sainthood for Edith Stein, the Catholic nun who was originally born a Jew, and who died in Auschwitz as a martyr. Liberal Protestantism has created a veritable theology of martyrdom around the figure of the minister Dietrich Bonhoeffer who sacrificed his life fighting against Hitler's tyranny. Israel has used the martyrdom of six million Jews to reinforce its own sense of solidarity, and reinforce the defense of its own political legitimacy. Janus Korczak, a martyr of the Warsaw ghetto, continues to be celebrated in North America, Europe, and the Middle East. In short, the political and religious saints, who have died willingly for their convictions, continue to be celebrated and

---

[8]Ibid, p. 129.

memorialized even by those who inhabit the social worlds that
celebrate the therapeutic ideology.

One could, in fact, make a case for the observation that martyrs are
particularly valued in a world that has become susceptible to the ethic
of self interest and personal fulfillment. As moral certainties crumble
under the influence of the therapeutic society there is a nostalgia and
growing fascination with those who sacrifice their lives willingly for
their convictions. As we feel ourselves becoming morally impoverished
we tend to idealize those who have proven their moral courage.

Towards A New Social Ethic: Neither the Hubris of the Therapeutic Self Nor the Fanaticism of the Martyr

It seems that, neither the therapeutic ideology nor the fanaticism
of martyrdom, exclusively, provides us with a valid basis for moral
conviction. One lacks the substance required for grounding our lives and
the other is too explosive and irrational a force which lends itself to
misuse. Can we have both in tandem? Can we hold on to both the
sensible, self interested, self appraising detachment of the therapeutic
moment and the burning, selfless certainties of conviction that come
with the martyr? We believe it is possible, with some important
qualifications.

Convictions are of two types. They can be linked to causes that are
either particularistic or universalistic. There are causes that serve the
interests of a particular ethnic, nationalistic, religious, or political
group and there are universalistic causes which Victor Turner has
called communitas (humanity), or Erik Erikson has termed the species
self (humankind). Unexpectedly, it is difficult to determine which of
these two has done more harm.

Particularistic convictions segment the world into ours and theirs.
They hierarchialize mankind into degrees of humanness, demonize
parts of humanity, grant moral warrants for cruel persecution and
murder in the name of group interest. Particularist causes are borne in
conflict, thrive in it, and are destroyed by it. Modern man in the
therapeutic age has been trained to be highly suspicious of such causes.
However, they have the advantage over universalistic causes in that
their aspirations and their appetites are limited.

Universalistic causes can even be more dangerous. They do not take
well to limits, and thus the possible destructive damage they can do is
much greater. When combined with deterministic theories of history or
with the assumed natural order, they destroy the possibility for
legitimate opposition. For who can stand up and challenge what is
presented as the march of history, the will of humanity or the
opportunity of the oppressed to free themselves? On what grounds does

one dare to do so? Universalistic causes usurp all the moral warrants and destroy the possibility of criticism. In the name of a higher good they devalue such parochial needs and interests as individual freedom and traditional family and community ties which are the requisites for self respect.

Both particularistic and universalistic causes in the end debase the self. They tend to crowd it out and delegitimate it in the name of promised posthumous victory. Strong convictions argue for the subordination of personal fulfillment to the goals of the cause. They attempt to convince the individual that authentic fulfillment consists in the triumph of the cause.

To all this the therapeutic ideology says no.

We believe rightfully so. The therapeutic era can be seen as a form of disenchantment with all causes beyond the individual. The retreat to self as the context in which to find the highest good is born out of a disappointment with causes. Introspection, the exploration of the inner world of feeling, the cultivation of private states and the communication of these inner space discoveries to others who value it become the essence of life. But what follows is disappointment. For however much the subjective world is changed and enriched by insight, and however much one's personal sphere of social engagements become more satisfying, the world at large remains much the same. In the end, it would appear that there is no way to make things a bit better in the world than by formulating a goal and devising a method to achieve it.

In this task, martyrs and other people of conviction have much to teach us. However, if their enthusiasms do not include self awareness and self respect they cannot become models of behavior for those in the enlightened world. And if they value themselves above their causes, they cannot become the heroes that are needed to validate the significance of conviction. We thus face a dilemma. We need a dedication to conviction to give values greater validity and we also need a remoteness from conviction in order to have the space to value the self. If our needs for both conviction and distance were simultaneous, we would be in greater trouble than we are. Fortunately for us we are capable of moving between the world of preoccupation with the self, and the world of causes. If in so doing our commitments lack single minded devotion or if our self preoccupations seem frivolous, then that is the price we must pay.

We are finished with causes that deny us, and dissatisfied with the world-creating potential of the therapeutic self. Until we develop a social philosophy that enables us to bridge the demands of self and the needs of an imperfect world we must continue to muddle through by first asserting the sovereignty of a sincerely noble cause, and then affirming the supreme importance of our own individual human needs.

The certainties which the Horst Wessel legend symbolized are no longer there for us, and although we long for these certainties, we see too clearly how we have been duped. However, there is little comfort in a world devoid of conviction. The best of the martyrs from the past teach us how serious and fateful our duties are, while the behavior models of the therapeutic world teach us our personal rights to happiness. This would appear to be our situation. We move between these two worlds, uncomfortably sensing the disparity between them, for they are indeed very different. Both personal rights and personal duties are necessary to maintain a balance which we can sustain. We don't seem to have much of a choice. We must continue to speak to our distraught and neurotic selves about the necessity of conviction even as we challenge our convictions with questions of self interest.

In this book we have attempted to analyze the link between convictions and the willingness to die for them. We have chosen martyrdom to explore this connection because martyrs poignantly symbolize both the power and the danger of strong conviction. The power of the martyr lies in his or her ability to validate controversial beliefs, to sacralize a cause, to inspire group cohesion and devotion and, ultimately, to make the structure of life meanings plausible.

The danger of the martyr is in the potential fanaticism of a zealot in the context of the nuclear age, and in the manipulation of the martyr narrative by evil craftsmen. These dangers are as real as the despair of a life without meaning. Torn between conflicting skepticism, admiration and fear, we contemplate those willing to die for their convictions.

Bibliography

(Books and Articles Consulted)

Abrahams, I. *Hebrew Ethical Wills*. Phil. Jewish Publication Society, 1948.

Aeschylus. *Prometheus Bound, The Suppliants, Seven Against Thebes, The Persians*. Middlesex, England; Penguin, 1961.

Agger, B. "Dialectical Sensibility II: Towards a New Intellectuality" *Canadian Journal of Political and Social Theory*. 1,2, Spring-Summer, 47-56, 1972.

Albury, W.R. "Politics and Rhetoric in the Sociobiology Debate," *Social Studies of Science*. 10, 4, No.: 519-539, 1980.

Histoire de Persecutions, Rona, "L'Erma" di Bretscheider, 1971.

Almond, G.A. & Verba, S. *The Civic Culture*. Boston; Little, Brown, 1965.

Alter, R. "The Masada Complex" *Commentary*. Vol. 56, No. 1, 19-24, July 1973.

Apfel, A. *Behind the Scenes of German Justice*. London; Lane, 1939.

Archives: The Wiener Library, 4 Devonshire St., London W.1

Author Unknown. *A History of the Most Distinguished Martyrs*. Philadelphia; A. Salisbury, 1831.

Bade, W. *Horst Wessel*. Berlin; D.U.V, 1933.

Bailey, F.G. *Gifts and Poison: The Politics of Reputation*, Oxford, Blackwell, 1971.

Bailey, F.G. *Strategies and Spoils*, Oxford, Blackwell, 1969.

Baldwin, D. "The Power of Positive Sanctions" *World Politics*, 19-38, 24 Oct. 1971.

Baron, S. *A Social and Religious History of the Jews*. New York; Columbia University Press, Jewish Publication Society, 1957

Becker, E. *The Denial of Death*. N.Y.; Free Press, 1975.

Becker, E. *Angel In Armour*. N.Y.; Free Press, 1969.

Becker, E. *The Structure of Evil*. N.Y.; Free Press, 1968.

Bell & Schaefer, (Martyr Mothers)

Bellah, R.N., Madsen, R., Sullivan, W.M., Surdeen, A., Tipton, S.M. *Habits of the Heart – Individualism and Commitment in American Life.* Berkeley; Univ. of California Press, 1985.

Bensieres, L. Pantheon des Martyres de la Liberte 940 B. 464

Bensley, R.L. *The Fourth Book of Macabees and Kindred Documents.* Cambridge, 1895.

Berger, P.L. *The Sacred Canopy: Elements of Sociological Theory of Religion.* New York; Anchor, 1969.

Berger, P.L. *A Rumor of Angels.* N.Y.; Anchor Doubleday, 1970.

Berger, P.L. "The Individual" unpublished paper, presented colloquium Boston Univ., 1983.

Berger, P.L. & Luckman, T. *The Social Construction of Reality.* N.Y.; Anchor Doubleday, 1967.

Bergesen, A.J. "Political Witch Hunts: The Sacred and the Subversive in Cross Cultural Perspective" *American Sociological Review.* Vol 42, No. 2:220-232, April 1977.

Bermann, C. *Scapegoat: The Impact of Death-Fear on an American Family.* Ann Arbor; Univ. of Michigan Press, 1973.

Berthoff, W. "Fiction, History, Myth" in Bloomfield, M.W. *Interpretation of Narrative; Theory and Practice.* Boston; Harvard Univ. Press, 1970.

Bethge, E. *Dietrich Bonhoeffer.* New York; Harper & Row. 1977.

Bethge, E. *Bonhoeffer, Exile and Martyr.* New York; Seabury, 1975.

Bickerman, E. "Les Maccabees de Malahas" *Byzantium.* 21, Fasc. 1: 63-83, 1951.

Bickerman, E. *From Ezra to the Last of the Maccabees.* N.Y.; Schocken Books, 1972.

Bidney, D. "The Concept of Myth and the Problem of Psychocultural Evolution" *The American Anthropologist,* Vol. 52 No. 1: 16-26

Binion, R. *Hitler Among the Germans.* N.Y.; Elseverm, 1976.

Bitner, E. "Radicalism and the Organization of Radical Movements" *American Sociological Review.* 28, No. 6, 928-940, Dec. 1963.

Black, M. *Models and Metaphors: Studies in Language and Philosophy.* Ithaca; Cornell Univ. Press, 1962.

Blum, A. *Theorizing.* Heinemann; London, 1973.

Blum, A.F. & McHugh, P. "The Social Ascription of Motives" *American Sociological Review,* Vol. 36, No.1, 98-109, Feb. 1974.

Blumstein, P.W. et.al. "The Honoring of Accounts" *American Sociological Review.,* Vol. 39 No. 4, 551-567, Aug. 1974.

Bosanquet, M. *The Life and Death of Dietrich Bonhoeffer.* New York; Harper, 1958

Bonhoeffer, D. *Letters and Papers from Prison.* New York; Macmillan, 1953.

Braver, S.L. "When Martyrdom Pays: The Effects of Information Concerning the Opponents' Past Game Behavior" *Journal of Conflict Resolution.* Vol 19, No. 4: 652-662, Dec. 1975.

Brodsky, A. *The Kings Depart.* New York; Harper & Row, 1974.

Bronowski, J. "The Logic of the Mind" *American Scientist.* 54: 1-14, 1966.

Brown, R.W. & Gilrain, A. "The Pronouns of Power and Solidarity," in Sebeok, T.A. *Style in Language,* New York; Wiley, 1960.

Bowra. *The Greek Experience.* London; Werdenfeld, 1961.

Bullough, E. "Psychic Distance as a Factor in Art and as an Aesthetic Principle" *British Journal of Psychology* Vol. 5, June 1912.

Bunker, E. "War Behind Walls: Racial Violence at San Quentin Prison" *Court Review.* Vol. 11, 5: 4-12, 1972.

Burke, Kenneth. *Permanence and Change.* Indianapolis; Bobbs-Merrill, 1965.

Byman, S. "Suicide and Alienation: Martyrdom in Tudor England," *Psychoanalytical Review.* Vol. 61, 3:355-373, 1974.

Byman S., "Child Raising and Melancholia in Tudor England" *Journal of Psychohistory.* Summer, Vol. 6 No. 1: 67-92, 1978.

Campbell, C. *Towards a Sociology of Irreligion.* London; Macmillan, 1971.

Campbell, D.T. "On the Conflicts Between Biological and Social Evolution and Between Psychology and Moral Tradition" *American Psychologist,* Vol. 30 No. 12, 1103-1128, Dec. 1975.

Camus, A. *Neither Victims or Executioners*

Camus, A. *The Rebel.* New York; Random House, 1956.

Cancian, F. *What Are Norms – A Study of Beliefs and Action in a Maya Community.* Cambridge Univ. Press, 1975.

Capps, D. "Lincoln's Martyrdom: A Study of Exemplary Mythic Patterns" in Reynolds, F. (Ed.) *Biographical Process,* 1976.

Cardenal, E. *The Gospel of Solentiname.* Maryknoll N.Y.; Orbis Books, 1971.

Carlson, M.L. "Pagan Examples of Fortitude in the Latin Christian Apologists" *Classical Philology.* p. 39, 1948.

Cassirer, E. *Language and Myth.* N.Y.; Dover, 1946.

Charles, R.H. *The Book of Jubilees.* London; Adam and Charles Black, 1902.

Charles, R.H. *The Assumption of Moses.* London; Adam and Charles Black, 1902.

Chevalier, J. "Myth and Ideology in Traditional French Canada: Dollard, The Martyred Warrior" *Anthropologica*. 21, 2, 143-175, 1975.

Chomsky, N. *Language and Mind*. N.Y.; Harcourt, Brace and World, 1968.

Choron, J. *Death and Western Thought*. New York; Collier Books, 1963.

Cirlot, J.E. *A Dictionary of Symbols*. London; Routledge and Kegan Paul, 1962.

Clark, F.S.J. *Eucharistic Sacrifice and the Reformation*. 2nd Ed., Oxford; Blackwell, 1967.

Cohen, A.A. *Arguments and Doctrines: A Reader of Jewish Thinking in the Aftermath of the Holocaust*. Reprints, 1970.

Cohen, G.D. "Messianic Postures of Ashkenazim and Sephardim" in *Leo Baeck Memorial Yearbook Nine*. New York; Leo Baeck, 1965.

Cohen, G.D. "Esau as Symbol in Early Medieval Thought" in Altmann, A. (Ed.) *Jewish Medieval and Renaissance Studies*. Cambridge; Harvard Univ. Press, 1967.

Cohen, Ronald, "Altruism: Human, Cultural, or What?" *Journal of Social Issues*, Vol. 28, (3), pp. 39-57, 1972.

Cohn, N. *Pageant of the Millenium*. London; Sechen and Warburg, 1957.

Coles, R. *Erik Erikson: The Growth of his Work*. Boston; Little Brown & Co. 1970.

Coser, L.A. "The Political Eunuch" in *Greedy Institutions*. New York; The Free Press, 1974.

Coser, L.A. "Social Types" in *The Pleasure of Sociology*. New York; Signet, 1974.

Craig, G.A. *The Germans*. N.Y.; G.P. Putnam and Sons, 1982.

Curtis, J. & Petras, J. *The Sociology of Knowledge: A Reader*. N.Y., Washington,; Praeger, 1970.

Cutter, F.C. "Suicide Themes in Visual Art" Omega, Vol. 3, pp. 1-24, 1972.

Daly, R. *Christian Sacrifice: The Judaeo Christian Background Before Origin*. Washington; Catholic Univ. Press, 1978.

Das. Grair. "Forms of Address and Terms of Reference in Bengali" *Anthropological Linguistics*. 10, No. 5: 19-31

Davis, M.S. & Schmidt, C.J. "The Obnoxious and the Nice" *Sociometry*. 40, 3: 201-213.

Delehaye, H. *Les Origines du Culte des Martyrs*. Brussels; Societe des Bollandistes, 1933.

Delehaye, H. *Sanctus: Essai sur le Culte de Saintes dans L'antiquite*. Brussels; Bollandist Fathers, 1927.

Dempsey, P.J.R. *The Psychology of Satre*. Cork University Press, 1950.

De Saussure, F. *Course in General Linguistics*. N.Y.; McGraw Hill, 1966.

Des Pres, T. *The Survivor, An Anatomy of Life in the Death Camps.* Oxford Univ. Press, 1976.

DeVries, A. et.al (Eds.), *The Dying Human.* Ramat Gan; Turtle Dove, 1978.

Douglas, M. *Natural Symbols, Explorations in Cosmology.* Vintage, 1973.

Dowd, D.L. *Pageant Maker of the Republic, Jacques Louis David and the French Revolution.* Lincoln, Nebraska; 1948.

Downing, J. "Jesus and Martyrdom" *Journal of Theological Studies.* N.S. Vol. XIV Pt. 2, 279-293, Oct. 1963.

Duncan, H.D. *Symbols and Social Theory.* N.Y.; Oxford Univ. Press, 1969.

Durkheim, E. *The Cult of the Self.*

Durkheim, E. *Suicide.* New York; Free Press, 1951.

Durkheim, E. *The Elementary Forms of Religious Life: A Study in Religious Sociology.* London; Allen & Unwin, New York; Macmillan, 1915.

Edmon, I. *Philosopher's Holiday.* New York; The Viking Press, 1938.

Egon, M. *Che: The Making of a Legend.* New York; Universe Books, 1969.

Edelman, M. *The Symbolic Uses of Politics.* Urbana III, Politics, 1964.

Eickelman, D.F. "The Art of Memory: Islamic Education and its Social Reproduction" in *Comparative Studies in Society and History.* Vol. 20, Part 4, October 1978.

Eliade, M. *Images and Symbols,* Hanville Press, 1952.

Eliade, M. *The Sacred and the Profane.* N.Y.; Harper, 1953.

Eliade, M. *The Myth of the Eternal Return.* London; Routledge and Kegan Paul, 1955.

Elliot, G. *Twentieth Century Book of the Dead.* Middlesex, England; Penguin, 1972.

Ellul, J. "Modern Myths" *Dialogues.* No. 23, 23-40, 1958.

Emmet, C.W. *The Third and Fourth Book of Maccabees.* New York; Macmillan, 1918.

Ephross, P.H. "Giving Up Martyrdom, It's Time for Practitioners to Assert Themselves" *Public Welfare.* Vol. 41, No. 2:27-33, 1983.

Erikson, E.H. *Young Man Luther: A Study in Psychoanalysis and History.* W.W. Norton, 1958.

Erikson, E.H. *Gandhi's Truth.* W.W. Norton, 1969.

Etzioni, A. *The Active Society,* New York; Free Press, 1968.

Euripides. "Iphigenia" in *The Complete Greek Drama.* New York; Random House, 1938.

Euripides. "Iphigenia in Aulis" in *The Complete Greek Drama.* New York; Random House, 1938.

Fairfield, L.P. "John Bale and the Development of Protestant Hagiography in England" *Journal of Ecclesiastical History*, Vol. 24, No. 2: 145-160, 1973.

Farmer, W. *Maccabees, Zealots, and Josephus.* New York; Macmillan, 1918.

Fenton, J.Y. (Ed.) *Theology and Body.* Philadelphia; Westminster Press, 1974.

Fischel, H.A. "Martyr and Prophet, (A Study in Jewish Literature)" *The Jewish Quarterly Review*, 37, 265-280, 363-386, 1946/47.

Foner, P.S. "A Martyr to His Cause, The Scenario of the First Labor Film in the United States" *Labor History.* Vol. 24 No. 1: 103-111, 1983.

Foxe, J. *The Book of Martyrs.* Newly Revised, 2 Vols. , London; J. Dayle, 1583.

Fraenkel, H. Maxwell, R. Dr. Goebbels, His Life and Death DD 247 G6733.

Fraser, J.T. "Temporal Levels: Socio-Biological Aspects of a Fundamental Synthesis" *Journal of Social and Biological Structures.* 1:339-355, 1978.

Franz, M.C.V. *The Passion of Perpetua.* Dallas, Texas; Spring Publications, 1979.

Frend, W.H.C. *Martyrdom and Persecution in the Early Church.* New York; Oxford, 1967.

Freud, S. *The Interpretation of Dreams.* London; Allen and Unwin, 1954.

From, F. *Perception of Other People.* N.Y.; Columbia Univ. Press, 1971.

Frost, C.J., Simone Weil: Self, God, and World, A Phenomenological Approach to the Experience of "Being Understood," Paper Presented at the Society for the Scientific Study of Religion, San Antonio, Texas, Oct. 26, 1979.

Fry, C. *The Lady is Not For Burning.* New York; Oxford, 1950.

Gall, N. "The Legacy of Che Guevara" *Commentary* 44:31-44, 1967.

Gardiner, J.K. "A Wake for Mother, The Maternal Deathbed in Women's Fiction" *Feminist Studies.* 4,2, 146-165, June, 1978.

Garrett, (martyr mother as response to father's pathology), 1975.

Girard, R. *Violence and the Sacred.* Baltimore & London; Johns Hopkins Univ. Press, 1972.

Goethe, J.W. *Iphigenia in Tauris.* Boston; Francis A. Niccolls & Co. 1902.

Goffman, E. *Strategic Interaction.* N.Y.; Oxford Press, 1970.

Goffman, E. *Interaction Ritual.* N.Y.; Doubleday, 1967.

Gordimer, N. & Dreyer, P. "Martyrs and Fanatics, South Africa and Human Destiny," *New Republic.* No. 7: 38-40, 1980.

Graves, R. *Greek Myths.* London; Cassel, 1969.

Guthrie, W.K.C. *The Greeks and Their Gods.* London; Methuen, 1968.

Grayzel, S. "The Confession of a Medieval Jewish Convety" *Historia Judaica.* 17, 89-120, 1955.

Green, M. *Dreams of Adventure, Deeds and Empire.* New York; Basic Books, 1979.

Griswold, W. "Cultural Legitimation and Social Change" *American Sociological Review.* 48: 668-680, 1983.

Hadas, M. & Smith, M. *Heroes and Gods: Spiritual Biographies in Antiquity.* New York; Freeport Press, 1965.

Hadas, M. *The Third and Fourth Books of the Maccabees.* N.Y.; Harper, 1953.

Haller, W. Foxe's Book of Martyrs and the Slect Nation. London; Jonathan Cape, 1963.

Haller, W. "The Tragedy of God's Englishmen" in *Reason and Imagination, Studies in History of Ideas 1680-1800,* N.Y.; Columbia Univ. Press, 1962.

Hamon, S.A. "Beyond Self-Actualization: Comments on the Life and Death of Stephen the Martyr" *Journal of Psychology and Theology.* Fall, Vol. 5, No. 4: 292-299, 1977.

Harrison, M. "Preparation for Life of the Spirit: The Process of Initial Commitment to a Religious Movement" *Urban Life and Culture.* 2:387:414.

Heiber, H. Goebbels DD247 G6H413

Heilbrun, A.B. "Distinctiveness of Maternal Control: A Further Link in a Theory of Schizophrenic Development" *Journal of Nervous and Mental Disease.* Vol. 154, 1: 49-59, 1972.

Hengel, M. *Judaism and Hellenism: Studies in Their Encounter in Palestine During the Early Hellenistic Period.* Philadelphia; Fortress Press, 1974.

Henn, T.R., *The Harvest of Tragedy.* London; Methuen, 1966.

Hernes, G., "Structural Change in Social Processes" *American Journal of Sociology.* Vol. 82 no. 3, 513-547, Nov. 1976.

Hesse, M. "Theory and Value in the Social Sciences" in *Actions and Interpretations. Studies in the Philosophy of the Social Sciences.* ed. C. Hookway, P. Pettit,. Cambridge; Cambridge Univ. Press, 1978.

Hewitt, J.P. & Stokes, R. "Disclaimers," *American Sociological Review.* Vol. 40 no. 1, 1-12, Feb. 1975.

Hibbard, H. *Bernini.* Middlesex England; Penguin, 1965.

Hick, J. *Death and Eternal Life.* London; Collins, 1976.

Hillman, J. *The Myth of Analysis: Three Essays in Archetypal Psychology.* Chicago; Northwestern Univ. Press, 1964.

Himmelfarb, G. "The New History" *Commentary.* 72-78, Jan 1975.

Hirn, Y. *The Sacred Shrine: A Study of Poetry and the Art of the Catholic Church.* London; Macmillan, 1912.

Hirschman, A.O. *Exit, Voice and Loyalty: Responses to Decline in Firms, Organizations and States.* Cambridge, Mass; Harvard Univ. Press, 1970.

Hopper, D.H. *A Dissent on Bonhoeffer.* Philadelphia; Westminster Press, 1975.

Hornstein, H.A. *Cruelty and Kindness: A New Look at Aggression and Altruism.* Prentice Hall, 1976.

Hovet, T.R. "Principles of the Hidden Life: Uncle Tom's Cabin and the Myth of the Inward Quest in Nineteenth Century American Culture" *Journal of American Culture.* 2,2, 265-270, Summer, 1979.

Howard, N. *Paradoxes of Rationality; Theory of Meta Games and Political Behavior.* Cambridge; MIT Press, 1971.

Hsin, W.P., "Martyr Yang, Kai, Hui will Always Live in Our Hearts" *Chinese Studies in History.* Vol. 12 No. 4: 54-60, 1979.

Huxley, A. *The Devils of Lonson.* London; Penguin, Hardmonsworth, 1971.

Huzinga, J. *The Waning of the Middle Ages.* London; Penguin, 1924.

Inoguchi, R., Nakajema, T. & Pineau, R. *The Divine Wind.* Annapolis, Md.; US Naval Institute Press, 1958.

Jackson, D.D. "Family Rules' The Marital Quid Pro Quo." *Archives of General Psychiatry.* 12: 589-596, 1965.

James, Daniel., *Che Guevera; A Biography.* New York; Stein and Day, 1969.

James, E.O. *Christian Myth and Ritual.,* London;, Murray, 1937.

Jan, Yun-Hua. "Buddhist Self Immolation in Medieval China" *History of Religions.* Vol 4 No. 1: 243-252, Summer, 1964.

Janowitz, Morris. "Sociological Theory and Social Control" *AJS.* vol. 81, 1; July 1975.

Jervis, R. *Perception and Misperception in International Politics.* New Jersey; Princeton Univ. Press, 1976.

Jochberg, E.C. *Das Jugendbuch Von Horst Wessel.* Stuttgart, Berlin, Leipsig; Union Deutshe Verlagsgefellschaft, 1933.

Johänsen, B. Nuclear Martyrs, Uranium Rush in Black Hills, S.D., *Nation.* Vol. 228. no. 14: 393-396, 1979.

Jung, C.G. *Symbols of Transformation.* N.Y.; Bolingnen, 1952.

Kanter, R.M. "Commitment and Social Organization" *American Sociological Review.* Vol 33 No. 4, Aug. 1968.

Katz, J. "The Jewish National Movement: A Sociological Analysis" in Ben Sasson & Hengin (Eds.). *Jewish Society Through the Ages.* London; Valentine Mitchell, 1971.

Katz, J. "Jewry and Judaism in the 19th Century" *Journal of World History.* No. 4, 881-900, 1958.

Katz, J.J. & Postal, P.M. *An Integrated Theory of Linguistic Descriptions.* Cambridge, Mass.; MIT Press, 1964.

Katz, J.J. *The Philosophy of Language.* N.Y.; Harper and Row, 1966.

Kaufman, W.A. *Tragedy and Philosophy.* Princeton, N.J.; Princeton Univ. Press, 1968.

Kelly, D.R. "Martyrs, Myths and Massacre: The Background of St. Bartholomew" *American Historical Review.* 78: 753-754, June 1973.

Kemper, T.D., "Social Constructionist and Positivist Approaches to the Sociology of the Emotions." *AJS,* vol. 87, 2 1981.

Kitagawam J.M. & Long, C.H. *Myths and Symbols.* Chicago; University of Chicago Press, 1969.

Klapp, O. "The Fool" *American Journal of Sociology.,* 55, 157-162, 1949.

Klapp, O. *Heroes, Villains and Fools.* Englewood Cliffs, New Jersey; Prentice Hall, 1962.

Klapp, O. "Social Types: Processes and Structure" *American Sociological Review.* Vol. 23, Dec. 1958.

Klapp, O. "The Clever Hero" *Journal of American Folklore.* Vol. 67, 21-34, 1954.

Klapp, O. *Symbolic Leaders: Public Dramas and Public Men.* Chicago; Aldine, 1974.

Klawiter, F.S. "The Role of Martyrdom and Persecution in Developing the Priestly Authority of Women in Early Christianity; A Case Study of Montanism" *Church History.* 49, 3, 251-261, Sept. 1980.

Knight, W.N. "Towards 'Archetype' in the Joseph Colombo Shooting" *The International Journal of Social Psychiatry.* 18, 4, 308-312, Winter, 1972.

Knowles, M.D. "Great Historical Enterprises: The Bollandists" *Transactions of the Royal Historical Society.* Series 5 Vol. VIII, 144-166, 1958.

Kolb, R. *For All the Saints.* Macon GA; Mercer Univ. Press, 1987.

Kuhn, A.J. "English Deism and the Development of Romantic Mythical Syncretism" *Modern Language Association.* Vol 71: 1099-1116, 1956.

Kulawiec, E. "Janusc Korzak, Educator – Martyr" *Intellect.* Vol. 102, N. 2358: 512-516, 1974.

Kursh, C.O. "The Benefits of Poor Communication" *Psychoanalytic Review,* 58,: 198-208, 1971.

Lakshman, S. *Sikh Martyrs,* DS 432 S5 L3

Lam, H. *Von Juden in Muenchen.* Munich; W.J. Cahnman, 1953.

Lambert, M.D. *Medieval Heresy: Popular Movements from Bogomil to Hus.* London; Edward Arnold, 1977.

Langholtz, L.V. *Hidden Myth: Structure and Symbolism in Advertising.* London; Heinemann, 1975.

Laqueur, W. *Guerrilla.* London; Weidenfield, 1971.

Laqueur, W. *Terrorism.* Boston; Little, Brown, 1977.

Laqueur, W. *Terrorism.* London; Sphere Books, 1980.

Lasch, C. *The Culture of Narcissism.* N.Y.; Warner Books, 1979.

Laswell, H.D., Lerner, D. & Sola Pool de, I. *The Comparative Study of Symbols.* CA; Stanford Univ. Press, 1952.

Lavelle, L. *The Dilemma of Narcissus.* London; George Allen & Unwin, 1973.

Lawyer, J.E. "Loyalty, Obligation and Resistance: The Christian Patriotism of Simone Weil" *Christian Scholastic Review.* Vol. 8, No. 3: 229-237, 1978.

Lebla, T.S. "Millenarian Movements and Resocialization" *American Behavioral Scientist.* 16: 195-217, 1974.

Leclerq, H. *Les Martyrs.* Paris; Tom IV, 1905.

Lefkowitz, M.R., "Motivations for St. Perpetua's Martyrdom" *J.A.A.R..* Vol. 44: 417-421, 1976.

Lerner, M.J. "All The World Loathes a Loser" *Psychology Today.* Vol. 5(1), 51-54,66., June 1971.

Lerner, M.J. *The Belief in a Just World: A Fundamental Delusion.* N.Y. & London; Penguin Press, 1980.

Lewis, Beth Irwin. *George Grosz: Art and Politics in the Weimar Republic.* Wisconsin; Univ. of Wisconsin Press, 1971

Lieberman, S. "Palestine in the Third and Fourth Centuries" *Jewish Quarterly Review.* 36: 329-370 & 47: 31-54; 46 & 47: 329-336, 1945, 1946, 1947.

Lieberman, S. "The Martyrs of Caesarea" *Annuaire de L'institut de Philologie et D'histoire Orientales et. Slavs.* 7: 430, 1939-1944.

Lifton, R. *New York Times Magazine Section.* New York City; June 4, 1979.

Lifton, R.J. *Death in Life, The Survivors of Hiroshima.* NY; Penguin, 1967.

Loades, D.M. *The Oxford Martyrs.* London; B.T. Batsford, (p 132), 1970.

Loney, J. "Family Dynamics in Homosexual Women." *Archives of Sexual Behavior,* 2.4, 343-350, Dec. 1973.

Lowenthal, M. *A World Passed By.* N.Y.; Harper and Row, 1933.

Lubin, A.J. "A Boy's View of Jesus" *Psychoanalytic Study of the Child.* Vol. 14: 155-162, 1959.

Lubin, A.J. *The Life of Van Gogh – Stranger on the Earth.* Great Britain; Paladin, 1975.

Lukacs, G. *The Historical Novel.* Boston; Beacon, 1962.

Lukacs, G. *History and Class Consciousness,* Cambridge, Mass; MIT Press, 1968.

Lyman, S. "The Glutton" in *The Seven Deadly Sins.* New York; St. Martin's, 1978.

Lyman & Scott. "On Accounts" *ASR.* 1971.

MacGregor, G.H.C. & Purdy, A.C. *Jew and Greek: Tutors Unto Christ.* New York; Scribners, 1936.

MacIntyre, A. *After Virtue.* Indiana; Univ. of Notre Dame Press, 1981.

Malone, E.E. *The Monk and the Martyr.* PhD Dissertation, Catholic University, (Photocopy), 1950.

Manson, T.W. Martyrs and Martyrdom, *John Rylands Library,* Vol. 39, 463-484, 1965.

Maranda, E.K. "The Logic of Riddles" in Marcudan P. & Maranda, E.K. *Structural Analysis of Oral Tradition.* Fayholtz, 1971.

Marsella, A.J. Dubanoski, R.A. & Mohs, K. "The Effects of the Father Presence and Absence upon Maternal Attitude" *Journal of Genetic Psychology.* Vol. 125, 2: 257-263, 1974.

Masaryk, T.G. *Suicide and the Meaning of Civilization.* Chicago; Univ. of Chicago Press, 1970.

McClendon, J.V. & Smith, J.M. *Understanding Religious Convictions.* Notre Dame; University of Notre Dame Press, 1975.

McClintock, C.G. "Social Values and their Definition, Measurement and Development" *Journal of Research and Development in Education.* Vol. 12 No. 1: 121-137, Fall 1978.

McDonald, G.W. "Deserved Victim and Martyr: Observer's Reactions" *Psychological Reports.* vol. 41 No. 2: 511-514, 1977.

McNamu, M.B. *Honor and the Epic Hero – A Study of the Shifting Concept of Magnanimity in Philosophy and Epic Poetry.* N.Y.; Holt, Rheinhart and Winston, 1960.

McQuire, M. "Testimony as a Commitment Mechanism in Catholic Pentecostal Player Groups" *Journal for the Scientific Study of Religion.* 16 (2) 165-168, 1977.

Meeropol, R.M. *We Are Your Sons.* Boston; Houghton Mifflin, 1975.

Menninger, K. *Man Against Himself.* New York; Harcourt Brace, 1938.

Merton, R.K. *Social Theory and Social Structure.* N.Y.; Free Press, 1968.

Merton, R.K. "Insiders and Outsiders" *American Sociological Review.* Vol. 78, No. 1, 9-47, July, 1972.

Methvin, E. *The Riot Makers: The Technology of Social Demolition.* New Rochelle, N.Y.; Arlington House, 1970.

Meyer, M.A. *Ideas of Jewish History.* N.Y.; Behrman House, 1979.

Mills, C.W. "The Competitive Personality" in Horowitz, I.L. (Ed.) *Power, Politics and People: The Collected Essays of C. Wright Mills.* New York; Oxford Press, 1963.

Mills, C.W. "Situated Actions and Vocabularies of Motive" *ASR*. 5, 904-13, 1940.

Mitchell – *Martyr Mother and early Socialization*, 1973.

Moore, G.F. *Judaism in the First Centuries of the Christian Era*, Vols. 1-4, Cambridge; Harvard Univ. Press, 1950.

Money, J. "Paraphilia and Abuse – Martyrdom: Exhibitionism as a Paradigm for Reciprocal Couple Counseling Combined with Antiandrogen" *Journal of Sex and Marital Therapy*. Vol 7 No. 2: 115-123, Summer 1981.

Mounteer, C. "Guilt, Martyrdom and Monasticism" *The Journal of Psychohistory*. Vol. 10, 1982-1983.

Muller, N. *Die Jude Katakombe Am Monteverde Zu Rom*. Leipzig; 1912.

Munro, D.H. "Concept of Myth" *Sociological Review*. Vol. 42m London; 115-132, 1950.

Muson, H. "Biology of Martyrdom" *Psychology Today*. Vol. 13 No. 6: 39, 1979.

Musurillo, H.A. *The Acts of the Christian Martyrs*. New York;, Oxford, 1972.

Neal, M.A. "Commitment to Altruism in Sociological Analysis" *Sociological Analysis*. Vol. 43 No. 1, 1-22, Spring, 1982

Nelson, C. "Stress, Religious Experience and Mental Health" *Catalyst*. Fall 1972.

Neumann, E. *The Great Mother*. London; Routledge & Kegan Paul, 1955.

Neumann, E. *The Archetypal World of Henry Moore*. London; Routledge & Kegan Paul, 1955.

Neusner, J. *Judaism: The Evidence of the Mishnah*. Chicago; Univ. of Chicago Press, 1981.

Nickelsburg, G.W. *Jewish Literature Between the Bible and the Mishnah*. Philadelphia; Fortress Press, 1981.

Nickelsburg, G.W. *Studies on the Testament of Moses*. Cambridge; Society of Biblical Literature, 1973.

Nigel, H. *Paradoxes of Rationality, Theory of Metagames and Political Behavior*. Cambridge; MIT Press, 1971.

Nisbet, R. *The Social Bond*. New York; Alfred A. Knopf, 1970.

Noss, J.B. *Man's Religion*. New York; Macmillan, 1957.

O'Grady, P. "Attributions of Strategies in the Prisoner's Dilemma Game." Dissertation Abstract, Ann Arbor, Michigan, 1970.

Oppen, B.R.V. "Bonhoeffer, Exile and Martyr." Bethge, E. *Catholic Historical Review*. Vol. 65, No. 1 90-91, 1979.

Otto, Rudolph. *The Idea of the Holy*. New York; Oxford Univ. Press, 1958.

Panichas, G.A. (Ed.) *The Simone Weil Reader*. N.Y.; David McKay, 1977.

Park, R.E. "The Marginal Man" *American Journal of Sociology*, 33: 200-206, 1928.

Parker, H.T., *The Cult of Antiquity and the French Revolutionaries.* Chicago; Harper, 1937.

Penner, H. "Is Phenomenology a Method for the Study of Religion?" *Buchnell Review.* 38: 29-54, 1970.

Peters. *The Concept of Motivation,* London; Routledge & Kegan Paul, 1958.

Peterson, R.T. *The Art of Ecstasy, Teresa, Bernini and Crashaw.* New York; Atheneum, 1970.

Petrement, S. *Simone Weil, A Life.* New York; Pantheon, 1976.

Pfeifer, R. *History of the New Testament Times with an Introduction to the Apocrypa.* New York; Harper, 1949.

Pfitzer, W.C. "Paul and the Agon Motif: Traditional to Athletic Imagery in the Pauline Literature" Supplemental *Novum Testamentum.* Leiden, Vol. 16, 1967.

Piaget, J. *The Moral Judgement of the Child,* New York; Collier Books, 1962.

Platt, J. "Social Traps" *American Psychologist.* Vol. 28, No.83: 641-651, Aug. 1973.

Pomeroy, S.B. *Goddesses, Whores, Wives and Slaves: Women in Classical Antiquity.* N.Y.; Schoken, 1975.

Propp, W. *Morphology of the Folktale.* Philadelphia; American Folklore Society, 1958.

Rahv, P. "Myth and the Powerhouse" *Partisan Review.* Vol. 20: p. 642, 1953.

Rappaport, A "Exploiter, Leader, Hero and Martyr: The Four Archetypes of the 2 X 2 Game" *Behavioral Science.* 12(2), 81-84, 1967.

Ravetz, J.R. "Tragedy in the Chilstory of Science" in *Changing Perspectives in the History of Science.* Leeds; Univ. of Leeds, 1973.

Reiff, P. *The Triumph of the Therapeutic.* New York; Harper & Row, 1966.

Reik, T. *Of Love and Lust,* New York, Farber & Strauss, 1957

Reik, T. *Masochism in Sex and Society.* N.Y.; Pyramid Books, 1976.

Reiss, C. *Joseph Goebbels: A Biography,* New York; Doubleday, 1948.

Reitman, E. *Horst Wessel: Leben un Sterber.* Verlag, 1932.

Ricciotti, G. *The Age of Martyrs.* Bruce Publishing, 1959.

Ricoeur, P. *Freud and Philosophy.* Conn.; Yale Univ. Press, 1970.

Riddle, D.W. *The Martyrs, A Study in Social Control.* Chicago; Univ. of Chicago Press, 1931.

Riesman, D., Glazer, N., Denney, R. *The Lonely Crowd.* New York; Anchor, 1954.

Ringgren, H. *Israelite Religion*. Philadelphia; Fortress Press, 1966.

Robbins, Thomas, "The Historical Antecedents of Jonestown" in: Moore, Rebecca & Fielding, McGehee (eds.) *The Sociology of Martyrdom*. Edward Mellon, in press.

Rose, H.J. *Gods and Heroes of the Greeks*. New York; Meridian Books, 1958.

Rosenberg, E. Ayman, B. & Sagarin, E. *Pictorial History of the World's Greatest Trials from Socrates to Eichman*. N.Y.; Crown, 1967.

Rothstein, D. "Culture, Creation and Social Reconstruction, The Socio-Cultural Dynamics of Intergroup Contact" *American Sociological Review*. Vol 37: 671-678, Dec. 1971.

Rumbaut, R.D. "Saints and Psychiatry" *Journal of Religious Health*. Vol. 15: 54-61, 1976.

Russell, J.B. "Interpretations of the Origins of Medieval Heresy" *Medieval Studies*. XXV, pp. 26-53, 1963.

Schegloff, E. & Sacks, H. "Opening Up Closings" in Turner, R. (Ed.) *Ethnome Theodology*. Harmondsworth, 1974.

Sawhill, J.A. *The Use of Athletic Metaphors in the Biblical Homilies of St. John Chripostom*. Princeton, 1928.

Schurer, E. *The History of the Jewish People in the Age of Jesus Christ*. Revised and Edited by Vermes, G., Miller, F., & Black, M. Edinburgh; T. & T. Clarck, 1973.

Schutz, A. *Collected Papers 1: The Problem of Social Reality*. The Hague; Nijhoff, 1962.

Shaw, G.B. *Saint Joan*. Baltimore; Penguin, 1954.

Shoham, G. *Social Deviance*. N.Y.; Gardner Press, 1976.

Schur, M. *Freud: Living and Dying*. International Univ. Press, 1972.

Schwartz, G. & Merten, D. "Social Identity and Expressive Symbols, The Meaning of an Initiation Ritual" *American Anthropologist*. 70: 1117-1131, 1968.

Schwartz, L. (Ed.). *Great Ages and Ideas of the Jewish People*. New York; Random House, 1964.

Shwartz, S. "Normative Influences on Altruism" in Berkowitz, L. (ed.) *Advances in Experimental Social Psychology*, New York; Academic Press, Vol. 10, pp. 222-279, 1974.

Shrewring, W. *The Passion of SS Perpetua and Felicity*. London; MM, 1931.

Simmel, G. "The Stranger" in Wolff, K.H. *The Sociology of George Simmel*. N.Y.C.; The Free Press, 1950.

Sluzki, C.E., Vernon, E. "The Double Bind As a Universal Pathogenic Situation" *Family Process*. 10: 397-410, 1971.

Smith, T.S. "Social Types" *American Sociological Review*. 39: 725-743, 1974.

Sophocles. *Electra and Other Plays.* Middlesex England; Penguin Books, 1953.

Sorokin, P. "Altruistic Love, Forms and Techniques of Altruistic and Spiritual Growth" *CS Review.* Vol. 6, No. 3, May 1977.

Spiegel, S. *(Group Imitation and Competition) The Last Trial: On the Legends & Lore of the Command to Abraham to offer Isaac as a Sacrifice.* N.Y.; Pantheon Books, 1967.

Spiegelberg, H. "On the I-Am-Me-Experience in Childhood" *Review of Existential Psychology and Psychiatry.* Vol.4, No.1, Winter 1964.

Stanton, M.D. "The Addict as Savior: Heroin, Death and the Family" *Family Process.* Vol. 16, No. 2: 191-197, June 1977.

Stein, H.F. "Judaism and the Group Fantasy of Martyrdom: The Psychodynamic Paradox of Survival Through Persecution" *Journal of Psychohistory.* Vol, 6. 2, 151-210, Fall 1978.

Stein, L. "Loathsome Women" *Journal of Analytical Psychology.* 1: 59-77, 1955-1956.

Steiner, G. *The Death of Tragedy.* London; Faber, 1961.

Stoneham, E.T. *Sussex Martyrs of the Reformation.* BR 1607 S73 1967.

Stokes, R. & Hewitt, J.P. "Aligning Actions" *American Sociological Review.* Vol. 41, No. 5,: 838-849, Oct. 1976.

Suden, B. "We're Drawing Young Blacks to Suicide" *Psychology Today.* (4), 3:24-28, 1970.

Sway, M.B. "Simmel's Concept of the Stranger and the Gypsies" *The Social Science Journal.* 18:1, 41-50, 1981.

Szasz, T.S. *Law, Liberty and Psychiatry.* N.Y.; Macmillan, 1963.

Tcherikover, V. *Hellenistic Civilization and the Jews,* Philadelphia; Jewish Publication Society, 1959.

Theodorson, G.A. Theordorson, A.G. *The Modern Dictionary of Sociology.* London; Crowell, 1969.

Thompson, G.V. *Foxe's Book of Martyrs: A Literary Study.* Ann Arbor, Mich.; University Microfilms, PhD Dissertation, 1974.

Thurston, H. & Altwater, D. (Eds.) *Butler's Lives of the Saints.* Great Britain; Palm Publishers, 1952.

Toth, M. "Toward a Theory of the Routinization of Charisma" *Rocky Mountain Social Science Journal.* 9.2: 93-98, April 1972.

Toynbee, A.J. *Greek Civilization and Character.,* N.Y.; Mentor Books, 1953.

Trevelyan, H. *Goethe and the Greeks.* New York; Octagon Books, 1972.

Trigg, R. *Reason and Commitment.* Cambridge University Press, 1923.

Trimble, V.C. "Masada, Suicide and Halakhah" *Conservative Judaism.* Vol. XXXI, No. 2, 45-55, Winter 1977.

Turner, J. "Toward a Sociological Theory of Motivation" *ASR.* Vol 52, pp. 15-28, 1 Feb. 1987.

Turner, V. *Drama, Fields & Metaphors.* Ithaca; Cornell University 1974.

Tytell, J. "Sexual Imagery in the Secular and Sacred Poems of Richard Crashaw" *Literature and Psychology,* 21, 1: 21-21, 1971.

Valentine, C. & Valentine, B. "The Man and The Panthers" *Politics and Society.* Vol. 2, 3: 273-286, 1972.

Von Franz, Marie-Louise. *The Passion of Perpetua.* Dallas, Texas; Spring Publications, 1980.

Vree, D. "Stripped Clean – Berrigans and Politics of Guilt and Martyrdom" *Ethics.* Vol. 85, No. 4: 271-287

Wagenheim. Martyr Mothers work outside the home, 1972.

Watzlawick, P., Burn, J.H. & Jackson, D.D. *Pragmatics of Human Communication: A Study of Interactional Patterns, Pathologies and Paradoxes.* CA; W.W. Norton, 1967.

Watzlawick, P. Weakland, J.H., & Risch, R. *Change: Principles of Problem Formation and Problem Resolution.* CA; W.W. Norton, 1974.

Weinstein, D. & Bell, R.M. Saints and Society, *The Two Worlds of Western Christendom, 1000-1700.* Chicago; Univ. of Chicago Press, 1982.

Weisberg, A. *The Accused.* N.Y.; Simon and Schuster, 1951.

Weil, S. *Gravity and Grace.* Arranged and Introduced by Gustave Thibon. London; Routlege & Kegan Paul, 1963.

Werner, E. "Traces of Jewish Hagiolatry" *Hebrew U.C.A.,* 51, 39-60, 1980,

Wexler, A. "The Early Life of Emma Goldman" *Psychohistory Review,* Vol. 8, No. 4: 7-21, Spring 1980.

White, B.R. "English Separatist Tradition from Marian Martyrs to Pilgrim Fathers" *History.* Vol. 58 No. 192: 99-100, 1971.

White, H.C. *Tudor Books of Saints and Martyrs.* Madison, Wis.; Univ. of Wisconsin Press, 1963.

Whorf, B.L. *Language, Thought and Reality.* Cambridge, Mass.; MIT Press, 1956.

Wilson, J. "Social Protest and Social Control" *Social Problems.* Vol. 24 No. 4,:469-481, April 1977.

Wilson, E. *Sociobiology.* Cambridge; Harvard Univ. Press, 1975.

Wilson, E. *On Human Nature.* Cambridge; Harvard Univ. Press, 1978.

Winslow, D.F. "Maccabean Martyrs, Early Christian Attitudes" *Judaism.* Vol. 23, No. 1: 78-86, 1974.

Wolman, B. "Interactional Group Psychotherapy with Schizophrenics." *Psychotherapy: Theory and Research.* 6(3) 194-198, 1969.

Wood, D. Pilisuk, M. & Uren, E. "The Martyr's Personality: An Experimental Investigation" *Journal of Personality and Social Psychology*, Vol. 25, 2: 177-186, 1973.

Workman, H. *Persecution in the Early Church*. New York; Apex Books, 1956.

Wrong, D.H. "The Oversocialized Conception of Man in Modern Sociology" *ASR*. Vol. 26, pp. 183-193, 2 April 1961.

Wykes, A. *The Nurenberg Rallies, Campaign Book Number 8*. London; McDonald, 1948.

Wyschograde, E. *The Phenomenon of Death – Faces of Mortality*. N.Y.; Harper, 1973.

X, Malcolm, *The Autobiography of Malcolm X*. N.Y.; Grove Books, 1964.

Zaner, R. "The Problem of Embodiment" *Phaenomenologica*. No. 17 1964.

Zaner, R. "The Radical Reality of the Human Body" *Humanities*. Vol. II, No. I: 73-87, 1966.

Zaner, R. "Merleau Pontys Theory of the Body as Etri-au-monde" *Journal of Existentialism*. Vol. 6, No. 21; 31-39, Fall 1965.

Zeitlin, S. *The Book of Jubilees*. Philadelphia; Dropsie College Press, 1939.

Zeitlin, S. *The Second Book of Maccabees*. New York; Harper, 1954.

Zeitlin, S. "The Legend of the Ten Martyrs and its Apocalyptic Origins" *The Jewish Quarterly Review*. pp. 1-17, 1953.

Zweig, P. *The Adventurer*. Princeton, N.J.; Princeton Univ. Press, 1974.

Index

Brown Judaic Studies

Brown Studies on Jews and Their Societies

Brown Studies in Religion

DATE DUE

FEB - 8 1999			